Special Praise for

Poised for Retirement

"Nayer's *Poised for Retirement* should appeal to everyone about to retire or who has recently retired. Not only will you gain insight from Louise's story, but also from those she interviews and from the great exercises that help people find happiness and calm during this huge life transition. This books speaks eloquently to the truth of the retirement journey."

Ravi Chandra, MD
Psychiatrist and Buddhist practitioner

"Few decisions are as momentous as when—and how—we retire. Louise Nayer gives us a compassionate and detailed account of her own journey, while including insights from ordinary retirees and experts. A must read for anyone considering this step"

Eleanor Vincent
Author of *Swimming with Maya: A Mother's Story*
(New York Times best-selling e-book)

"Louise Nayer's *Poised for Retirement* reinforces the fact that everyone needs to think about when and whether they are going to retire. My research for *The Bitch in Your Head: How to Finally Squash Your Inner Critic* confirmed how vital it is to have a post-retirement plan so 'the Bitch' doesn't make you feel depressed because you are 'old and over the hill.'"

Jacqueline Hornor Plumez, PhD
Author of *The Bitch in Your Head:
How to Finally Squash Your Inner Critic*

Poised for Retirement

POISED *for*
RETIREMENT

Moving from Anxiety to Zen

Louise Nayer

For Judy,
To a wonderful
retirement! All best,
Louise

CRP
CENTRAL RECOVERY PRESS
LAS VEGAS

Central Recovery Press (CRP) is committed to publishing exceptional materials addressing addiction treatment, recovery, and behavioral healthcare topics.

For more information, visit www.centralrecoverypress.com.

Publisher: Central Recovery Press
             3321 N. Buffalo Drive
             Las Vegas, NV 89129

22 21 20 19 18 17   1 2 3 4 5

Library of Congress Cataloging-in-Publication Data
Names: Nayer, Louise, author.
Title: Poised for retirement : moving from anxiety to Zen / Louise Nayer.
Description: Las Vegas, NV : Central Recovery Press, [2017]
Identifiers: LCCN 2017007551 (print) | LCCN 2017017690 (ebook) | ISBN 9781942094401 | ISBN 9781942094395 (alk. paper)
Subjects: LCSH: Nayer, Louise. | Retirees--United States--Biography. | Retirement--United States.
Classification: LCC HQ1063.2.U6 (ebook) | LCC HQ1063.2.U6 N39 2017 (print) | DDC 646.7/9--dc23
LC record available at https://lccn.loc.gov/2017007551

Photo of Louise Nayer by Jarda Brych. Used with permission.

Every attempt has been made to contact copyright holders. If copyright holders have not been properly acknowledged please contact us. Central Recovery Press will be happy to rectify the omission in future printings of this book.

Publisher's Note: This book contains general information about the anxiety and emotional challenges related to retirement. The information is not medical advice. This book is not an alternative to medical advice from your doctor or other professional healthcare provider.

Our books represent the experiences and opinions of their authors only. Every effort has been made to ensure that events, institutions, and statistics presented in our books as facts are accurate and up-to-date. To protect their privacy, the names of some of the people, places, and institutions in this book may have been changed.

Cover and interior design by Sara Streifel, Think Creative Design

I would like to dedicate this book, first of all, to my parents who showed me you can follow your dreams, to my sister for her constant love and support, to my children and grandchildren, the hope of the future, and, finally, to my husband, Jim, who is always at my side cheering me on.

I   I   I

To our precious dog, Penny, who passed away in 2014. Sometimes I still imagine you at the top of the stairs, waiting for us to come home. You will always be at home with us. To our new dog, Ella, you bring us love and comfort as we navigate the new waters of retirement.

Table of Contents

Author's Note

In order to maintain the confidentiality of those I interviewed, I did not use last names. I also tried to get a cross-section of the population—men, women, single, those with partners, high-income, low-income, and those who still need to do part-time work to pay the bills (many retirees find they cannot manage on their retirement alone). It is by no means representative of everyone in America, but I do hope most readers will find pieces of themselves in the lives of those included here.

- Jim, senior center director and now part-time history teacher
- Betsy L., administrator for a newspaper
- Leslie, community college instructor and writer
- Pamela, Episcopal priest
- John R., physician
- Steve, chief operating officer for a men's club
- Ken, art history professor and museum curator
- Emily, data security and privacy professional
- Betsy E., family services manager
- Claire, nurse practitioner, now part-time nurse
- Barry, city planner

- Sonia, teacher and now part-time caregiver

- John L., business executive

- Anna, accountant

- Eleanor, corporate editor and now part-time writer

- George, machinist at city newspaper

- Dixie, Montessori teacher

Acknowledgments

I am eternally indebted to the people I interviewed for this book. Thank you all for taking the time to talk with me about such personal feelings surrounding your retirement and for your wisdom. You are the true heroes of the book, as you navigate a new part of life with great courage.

I also want to thank friends and family who read drafts of this book and gave me help and inspiration, especially Melissa Kite, Anne Nayer, Jim Patten, Dixie Morse, Ginny Lang, and Kenneth Silver. Thank you to those who offered their professional expertise: Jennifer Lane, Dr. Jacqueline Hornor Plumez, and Dr. Chandra.

Thank you to the San Francisco Writer's Grotto and everyone there who gave me shelter from the storm: you created a safe and generous second home for me.

To my agent, Janet Rosen, a big thank you for all you have done for me and for finding a home for this book.

I also want to thank Central Recovery Press and everyone who has helped shepherd this book to completion. I am honored to be one of your authors. Thank you also to Patrick Hughes and all the work you do to get this book out into the world. Finally, thank you to my editor, Nancy Schenck, for your warmth, your skill, and your belief in this book.

Introduction

I'm sixty one years old. I walk to the Social Security Office, past Manuela's Beauty Salon and the smells of tacos in the Mission District of San Francisco. As I enter the building, a security guard sits at a big table, looks up briefly, and then goes back to reading the paper. My number—twenty-five—is spit out of a metal machine. The woman next to me nervously shifts back and forth in her seat. A man across from me has fallen asleep and is about to snore. The wall monitor displays "Thinking about Retiring" in big black letters across the top of the screen with photos of a beautiful lake and trees underneath. I don't think many people in this room will have *that* kind of retirement, lying on lawn chairs near an emerald mountain lake surrounded by pine trees. They look worried and haggard like many of the aging population in twenty-first century America. But who knows?

I pull *The McGraw-Hill Reader* for my English 1A college classes out of my huge red purse and begin reading "Unplugged: The Myth of Computers in the Classroom." Even though I've taught this essay many times before, the words "hypermedia," "linear," and "multimedia" run together, vanish into the ether. I usually need to reread everything before class. School starts in three days. I must cram. I also look achingly at my small, black writing journal—also in my purse—my creative life beckoning me from the bottom of a mess of old Bic pens, quarters for the parking meters, and crumbs left over from a sugar cookie. I want to finish a piece of writing I have been working on, but now is not the time.

When is the time?

What will my monthly payment be at sixty-two? I've been obsessively punching numbers into my calculator for over a year, trying to decide if, in fact, I *can* leave my job. It's now January. I'm thinking of retiring in May after teaching for twenty-seven years at community colleges. I spent thirteen of those years as a part-timer at two schools—"freeway flying" like many underpaid part-timers do—driving thirty miles each way between campuses, stacks of papers sliding back and forth as I navigated Highway 280. Now, I'm dragging myself everywhere. I feel tired. Body-soul tired.

"How did I get this old?"

"Just keep breathing," my husband, Jim, six years my senior, teases. Some people smile and say, "Sixty is the new forty." But lately, as I lie on the couch, trying to soothe my sore neck, I fully inhabit my sixty-one-year-old body with its aches and pains and thinning eyebrows, wrinkles, sun spots, and gray hairs that sprout in an unseemly round patch at the back of my head.

But maybe—just maybe—if I leave my job, I will be one of those young sixty-one-year-olds. I'll bike up hills, walk half-marathons, and join the Dolphin Club and jump into the chilly water of the San Francisco Bay with those hardy octogenarians and feel the energy surging through my system. I'll write and teach workshops at my house. I'll take classes.

"Number twenty-five?" That's me. I stuff my book in my purse and follow a middle-aged, dark-haired woman through a door that locks behind us and down a narrow hallway to her cubicle. She's nice but officious. When she pushes a button on the printer, my "award" slides out of the machine and into my hands. This is the final piece of evidence I need to make my calculations. I say goodbye, put the printout in my purse, and walk back to my car. I have a lot to think about. Can I do this? Will I do this?

If I want a different life, if I want to leave my job and still be healthy—mind, body, soul healthy—then now is the time.

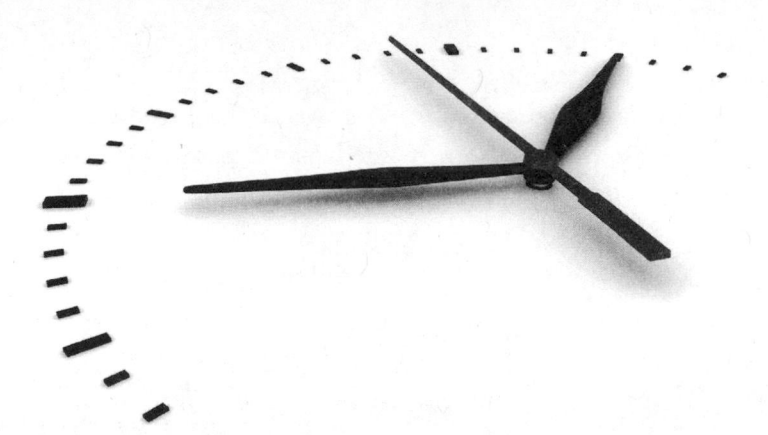

JANUARY

Making the Decision

How do we decide to finally make the decision to leave our jobs? Is it always a "rational" decision? What fears surface? Has exhaustion set in? What could a post-retirement life look like? How can we calm ourselves during this time?

As I get closer to making the decision to retire from my full-time teaching job, my inner voices plague me with their fearful, garbled sounds. Two, three, four more years would make a big difference in my pension. I'm lucky to have a pension, but most people stay until they're sixty-three when the pension goes up. Can't I just stay longer? If I leave in five months will I have enough money for housing and food and maybe a vacation? My husband retired a few years ago as director of a senior citizen's center. He has social security. We can just make it; I think and calculate endlessly. But can we?

I have strange dreams night after night. I dream I'm losing my fingers on my right hand, making it impossible for me to write, and writing is my passion. I dream of ghosts with long, white hair and protruding teeth going up and down in huge elevators. They're beckoning to me with their skinny, knobby fingers. I'm scared and race down the stairs, my perspiring hands almost slipping off the bannister. I hear their witchy laughs echoing off the walls. I wake up drenched in sweat. The next night, I dream of drowning. I dream of frogs eluding my attempt to grasp their slippery, green bodies. I dream of words, words moving fast on a player piano, scrolling so rapidly on rolls of papers I can't write them down and wake up frustrated, my potentially brilliant thoughts vanishing as I rise to the loud buzz of the alarm clock and the smell of coffee. Sometimes I spend my early morning hours searching for a stack of papers I graded until 1:00 a.m. and left in a pile on some surface in the house.

While sitting on our red couch, with the television playing *Law and Order* marathons, I pull out calculators and endlessly, more like obsessively, look at what money will come in and go out. Credit. Debit. Credit. Debit. Credit. Debit. The words spin above my head in a surreal cartoonish loop.

I think about my job and what it will be like to actually leave. Will I miss my community at work? Will I miss the quick talks between classes? My life is so enmeshed with those of my coworkers. I grew up in a housing development, Peter Cooper Village, in New York City. When I was a young child, I remember holding on to my mother's skirt, impatiently waiting for her to stop chatting incessantly to the many friends she met on the serpentine road that snaked through our complex. Now I understand how important those conversations were to her, that constant connection with others and how much they all shared living in the same community.

I'll miss talking with my colleagues about the latest novels, poetry, memoirs, and plays I've been teaching. I'll miss asking about their partners, children, grandparents, or trips they're about to take. I'll miss their "Hang in there," when things are difficult or their congratulations at good news like when my children were born, my books published, or when I finally got tenure. I'll miss the constancy of seeing the same people every day. How will I find a new community? What will I do each day without the structure of a job? I mentally talk to my parents who have passed away. Should I retire now?

My mother's biological father, a social worker in the Salvation Army, left the family and emptied the bank account when my mother was nine. Though my mother and my father had a comfortable life— stable professional jobs, a beautiful apartment in Greenwich Village, money for a trip every year, new clothes, tickets to plays, concerts, and a savings account—the underlying dread about money pervaded everything, a huge black umbrella over my head. It could always rain. You always need to save for a rainy day.

Most people have money fears. Some people on social security often pray their food stamps will cover the necessary three meals a day or a relative or friend will take them in if they can't afford housing. People on disability insurance desperately hope for cost of living raises each year while those who have millions invested worry when the market will take another dive. Jennifer Lane, an award-winning financial advisor from Boston who has helped countless people, says, "You need to have a clear discussion with yourself about what you can or cannot afford." She also says that before you retire you need to track your expenses. *All your expenses.* "What will you need to make you happy?" she asks clients. But have I done that really well? How about the pocketbook-sucking lattes I get at local cafes? Or the expenses I never factor in such as car repairs? We have a 2003 car. Things have literally started falling off the car—one plastic piece at a time.

Have I thought this out?

I sit cross-legged on my bed and hold a private financial séance, listening for knocks from my Depression-era mother, ever practical. "I never bounced a check," she would say. And, she grew up in Salvation Army homes and put herself through nursing school.

I *have* bounced checks, especially in my early twenties living "from hand to mouth" as a starving poet—though my parents could have bailed me out of a medical crisis or an emergency. Not everyone has a back up. Most don't. Also, living in the twenty-first century is especially costly. Rent or mortgage can easily cost half your take-home pay. Tuition has risen astronomically, and many students have debt they may not be able to pay off in a lifetime. Paying for our technological devices—cell phones, cable TV, computers, tablets—and the cost of healthcare also eat into our income in ways that couldn't even have been imagined fifty years ago. Who knew we would be shelling out a lot of money every month to be looking at handheld and movie theater–sized screens?

After I retire, I envision my bills going to collection agencies. Then I take a deep breath and wait for my chair to magically rise from the floor, asking my parents' permission to retire like a four-year-old child. "Mom, Dad, should I do this? Am I screwing up my life by leaving now?" They passed away, but I know they are listening.

I listen to my husband, sister, family, and friends.

I listen to my aching neck. I want to retire before my neck problems get even worse, and I might need a risky operation. I've graded too many papers; cervical five or six are permanently damaged. Compression. Arthritis. "A normal neck would not have this," my chiropractor says, pointing out the tilt to the right and all the degeneration. "Your neck is as fragile as a teacup." Yes, if I stay two or three more years my pension will go up, but is it worth it? As my writer-friend, Eleanor says, recently retired as an editor for a hospital, "There is a trade-off between getting more money by staying another few years and the time you have left—a question that becomes more poignant and urgent as we get older." Retirement is different than switching jobs when you were younger. Retirement, especially in your sixties or later, is the last chapter of a life. What will this chapter be?

At City College, where I work, hundreds of emails pop up on my computer screen every day. But one email that appears too regularly is bolded in all caps: **SAD NEWS TO REPORT.** Someone has died. I see those emails and swallow hard before I open them. I pray it's not a good friend. Last year, it *was* a good friend. His son went to high school with my older daughter. He died two weeks before he retired. He and his wife had tickets to go to Japan. His death could not be predicted, as many aren't. It was unexpected, sudden and shocking. He was supposed to live a long time. He was active, ate well, and looked forward to traveling, painting, and writing. It seemed so unfair.

Heart attacks, cancer, "death from unknown causes." Some people die in the classroom, assaulted by fluorescent lights, chalk in hand. Nurses rush up steep stairs to Cloud Hall or the science building with defibrillators. One man died the other day in the classroom. He just crumpled, collapsed on the linoleum floor. He didn't even make it to the hospital.

Many people now will work until they are six feet under.

Some people *want* to stay at their jobs until they drop. Many will have no choice because of their finances.

Though it's admirable, and maybe I *should* die while giving a lesson plan, I don't *want* to die in the classroom.

I want a chance at another life.

I see a vision of my Uncle Louis, my mother's brother. He worked as a stationary engineer for Norwich Pharmacy. He had a sturdy body and wide smile. He was such a strong and confident man, the father-surrogate who cared for my sister and me on a dairy farm in the blink-of-an eye town of Sherburne, New York. We stayed with him for nine months after my parents were severely burned in a gas explosion when I was four.

I learned at four that life *can*—and often does—change instantaneously. It's important to love your life, now. Pamela, retired as an Episcopal priest, says people need to ask the questions, "What do I want to do? Where do I want to be?" The writer Alice Walker, in *Temple of My Familiar*, says, "Keep in mind always the present you are constructing. It should be the future you want."

I keep those words on my refrigerator and look at them every day.

When Uncle Louis was fifty-eight, he and my aunt bought a trailer and parked it near a lake. This was to be their time—to relax in the sunshine during those tranquil upstate New York summers, spending time with the children and grandchildren, and everyone dipping their bodies into the cool water crowded with minnows. To my aunt's and his family's anguish, that time never came. He died at sixty; keeled over on his front lawn one year after he retired.

My mother rarely cried. Yet, just after my uncle died, she was ironing in the small kitchen of our apartment on 12th Street in New York City, tears streaming down her face. She didn't want me to hug her, so I just stood there, helplessly and silently. Perhaps she learned at an early age to build a wall around her heart when her father walked out or maybe after her face was so terribly burned. The stoicism she learned as a child got her through life. One day, when I was playing Exodus on the piano she said, "I don't like anything in a minor key." Maybe if she cried or truly showed her grief, her tears would have flooded the entire world.

But, I am not my Uncle Louis. I stopped smoking at twenty-eight. I have no heart condition that I know of; have no cancer; and certainly don't want to be radiated by a full body scan to show all my warts and growths. However, who knows what lurks inside our bodies or how many more years each of us has left on this planet?

Is the decision to retire always carefully thought out?

Do most of us really have enough money to live well into our nineties? Planning is always better, and some people have planned wonderfully for their golden years. All children should be taught to save at an early age. The younger you save, the better. My tax accountant, Julie, recently said she should run workshops for twenty-one year olds to show them how saving only fifty dollars a month now will be big money by the age of sixty-five. When my husband was young, the schools gave out little piggy banks and taught the children about saving. In the best of all possible worlds, young people should start retirement accounts as early as they can—in fact, some do. Jennifer Lane advises that pre-retirees should track all their expenses for one year, from lattes to pet food, and account for inflation and rising medical expenses. She says people should know what their life actually costs.

Yet, life doesn't always follow the plan. The brother of a friend of mine had a lot of money; he was an executive for a renowned ad agency in New York City, but his daughter had mental heath problems. They had the means to send her to the best facilities, which cost enormous amounts of money, and today she's doing well. For that, they are eternally grateful. However, their money situation is not so good in old age. Who could have predicted that?

Some will save responsibly and others won't.

Many of us will want to leave our jobs for all sorts of reasons and then, if necessary, figure out a way to survive.

John R., a retired physician, thought he would work much longer than sixty-four years old, though not for financial reasons as he was quite comfortable financially when he retired. Medicine was his beloved profession. "Retiring was not an intellectual decision." After his father died, he said, "I became more reflective. Things just accumulated." He suddenly got annoyed when interns called in the middle of the night, asking what to do about a patient. He used to be happy to take those calls. "I didn't want to be in a war zone anymore," he said. "I used to love being in the middle of everything, but no more." He talks about emotional burnout and how his emotional bank account was overdrawn. He felt depleted, physically and emotionally. Before, when he went on vacations, he was always anxious to get back, to get recharged by his workplace adrenaline rush. But, suddenly, he wanted to stay on vacation longer. That was a sign. He went with his wife to a mindfulness meditation group and now meditates five days a week. He cites David Brooks, a political commentator who wrote the *New York Times* piece, "The Moral Bucket List."[1] As we get older, Brooks says, it's more important to live for your eulogy—that is, who you are, what your core values are, and how you have treated other people—rather than your resume, what you have done and achieved. John R.

---

1   David Brooks, "The Moral Bucket List," the *New York Times,* April 11, 2015.

became more inward, more self-reflective. "When I took a walk, I began to look at the sky and trees. I hadn't done that before."

Steve, who retired at sixty-five as the chief operating officer (COO) of a prestigious men's club, said, "I hit a wall. I knew I wanted to leave." The usual tenure for COO was five years. He had stayed for twenty years. He turned the club around to great success and sometimes worked sixty to seventy hours a week. When the club had retreats, he often worked from 6:00 a.m. to 1:00 a.m. making sure everything ran smoothly, from ordering food for four hundred people to ensuring there was good access to medical care and personnel. But, he became exhausted. He had worked since he was eleven years old.

Hitting a wall seems to be a theme. Some people I spoke with talked about difficult bosses. Claire, a nurse practitioner at a huge urban hospital, said she had a series of nightmare supervisors. "There were explosive confrontations every day. The expectations of how many patients to see in a day were not reasonable or acceptable. I did not want to get pushed that hard." Some people talk about a difficult boss as "long-time torture." As people get older, they don't want to put up with as much conflict as they did when they were younger and, if possible, they plan a way out.

Moreover, as people age, burnout becomes more common. My husband, Jim, started working in his father's meat business at twelve years old. Later, and for many years, he worked with independent and developmentally disabled seniors in an integrated program that he started. Although he loved his job and was dedicated to all the seniors, he had an "empathy burnout" when he turned sixty-five and hung in there until he was sixty-six to get a larger social security check. He checked off days on the calendar to help him get through those last few months. Jim felt like an unhappy kid at summer camp, aching to go home. He felt oppressed and aggravated every day.

Jim never wanted to be part of the "detached concern" movement that social workers were taught to follow. He was endlessly concerned and loving, always helping people with activities and assisting clients in wheelchairs when transferring for transportation and personal needs. They were not "the other" or "the frail elderly" as some in gerontology proclaimed. His clients became our family friends: Uncle Bill, a mental-health patient, artist, and gardener, planted gorgeous flowers with our small daughters, Sarah and Laura, in our backyard garden and taught them how to draw. He held them on his lap as he showed them how to sketch butterflies, flowers, houses, cats, and dogs. Sarah wrote about him for her college entrance essay. At the end of her essay, she said that society might not see her Uncle Bill as a successful person, but, to her, he would always be famous. We were all there by his hospice bed when he died.

Josee, blind and brilliant, wrote poetry in classes I taught at the senior center. She was a psychologist, trained at the Paris-Sorbonne, and an artist. She showered us with endless wisdom. Another blind person, Will, who often came to the senior center, didn't believe Josee was blind since she navigated the world so well. One day, though, my husband saw her cross Masonic Avenue in San Francisco. She was walking diagonally across the huge boulevard, cars almost hitting her and screeching to a halt since the light had just turned red. She was definitely blind.

Both Uncle Bill and Josee sat at our dinner table for Thanksgiving. Jim loved his job and the clients.

But five months before he retired, Jim said he, too, had hit a wall.

Even though I have hit a wall mentally and physically, my mental flip-flops continue to plague me. I'm getting out earlier than I thought I would. I feel like I'm not being prudent. Unlike others who have paid off mortgages and planned for life's incidentals and emergencies better, I'll have to bring in some money after I retire.

Is this a foolish decision?

Fears Surface: How Will My Decision Impact Others?

For many of us, deciding to retire affects not only us but also other family members, partners, spouses, children, and, perhaps, friends. In my situation, I knew I would need to continue to do some type of work to make ends meet or take in students at our home, yet it still wouldn't be nearly as much money as I was earning at my job. I worried about my children who were not quite "launched" in their own lives and careers.

Fears about my children surface.

My children are now adults, twenty-five and twenty-seven, on their own paths.

If I retire from City College at sixty-two, I won't be able to keep my younger daughter on my healthcare plan because it's too expensive. During her childhood, she always could go to the doctor and quickly get medicine, if needed. She had three strep throat infections in third grade, the year her classroom was filled with furry animals: hamsters, doves, and gerbils. We think her allergies might have compromised her immune system, making her more susceptible to strep. But now, what if she needs an operation? Will her new plan offer her good enough care? And, my older daughter just lost her healthcare insurance and called from New York City with a horrible stomachache. What if it's appendicitis? *I will not worry. I will not worry*. I repeat to myself.

Then I wake up from a dream where I'm wading knee-high through muddy water. There's no one around. I'm trying to get to a Kaiser facility—the nearest HMO. Is this a premonition? A nurse-friend said my daughters could go on Medicaid. A hospital would take them. There are free clinics. There are angels out there. I see their wispy wings. I try to hear angel songs in my mind.

Retirement planners often warn about this—to have more saved—because children sometimes need a lot of help in these terribly uncertain times. It's tough out there for the next generation.

Can we help our children financially should they need it if I retire now? They're both going to go back to graduate school. Jim and I have offered to pay their rent while in school. We need to make sure we can bring in enough money for that. We started renting our home short-term and vagabonding at other friend's houses, so grateful for their offers, or sometimes staying in our garage. That helps enormously. But how long can we schlep our belongings from place to place? After three years of doing this, we've started to feel like Willy Loman, from Arthur Miller's play *Death of a Salesman*, who doesn't know what bedroom he's in when he wakes up. We're lucky to have a house to rent out, and the money has been a godsend. We're proud that our daughters chose to continue with their education and hopefully find careers they love.

However, our children, like so many of this new generation, will have crushing student debt. But will they get jobs? For the top investors, the economy is doing well; yet, most of us struggle to pay the bills. Money is always a worry. For Sonia, in her seventies, she has some savings but still works every day, part-time as a caregiver for a woman with Alzheimer's. "I can never completely retire," she says, "but I like working." She was not one of the savers—as financial experts would advise—who started putting money away in their twenties and let it grow and grow. For many of us, the creed of the 60s and 70s was to live for *now*. Saving for the future was square. Anyone over thirty was not to be trusted. But circumstances conspired and left her with only $900 in social security benefits: a husband who insisted she quit her teaching job at a time when women usually stayed home with the children and a divorce, all meant she, like millions of others, did not get a pension in old age.

One day she woke up and realized she needed to save and could actually save something every month. It was not enough, however, to allow her to completely retire, but she says, "I adore teaching." She has made a huge difference in the lives of so many young people, such as the young boy who was marginalized, as some children are, by his peers and sat on her lap and cried as she held him. She also advises people "to do what you love and be kind and help as much as you can." Although her money situation is not ideal, she does live in a rent-controlled apartment, has some savings, and has had a rich life of helping others. Fortunately, her health is still good. Is she secure financially? No. Many baby boomers are in the same position.

Even people with a lot of money worry about taking care of themselves or other family members. Worry about money seems to be imbedded in our DNA. A friend's husband, John L., retired with more than enough money at the young age of fifty-three as a top executive of a corporation. He said he had missed his daughter's childhood with his long work hours and constant global travel. By retiring, he could finally be part of her middle- and high-school life. When they lived in Brussels, he said, he got into a taxi to go on one of his many trips, and his daughter blurted out, "Don't go, Daddy, don't go." Now, as he says, he has "blessed time" with his daughter. He has enough money, but the fear of *not* having enough money still makes him anxious. "Even though we're fine financially, I make budgets for the whole year; I micromanage our finances. You never know what will come up." His daughter is now about to go off to college.

My nephew George, a machinist on disability because of a back injury and an endlessly kind and helpful person, was forced to retire from a job he loved. For now, he's okay financially, and his wife, my niece Laura, still works full-time as a certified public accountant, but when his workman's compensation runs out, things will be tougher for both of them. His retirement affects my niece as well. She might like to retire soon. They need the income. How will they manage? The pain in his back is excruciating. He makes the best of his life with great courage and kindness. Somehow, they will work it out. For many, our decisions affect not only us, but also others in our constellation of people.

∎　∎　∎

What are ways to help with the decision? To calm yourself? There are numerous ways to find your peaceful center during this transition. For me, self-hypnosis has served me well for years. I was lucky to find a good hypnotist, Isabel Gilbert, referred by a friend who had been assaulted. He felt terrified to walk the streets after the attack. She made him a tape, which he played over and over again until he could go out and feel calm. That tape changed his life.

I had panic attacks, once at twenty-one and later at forty-two, probably stemming from a combination of genetics and early childhood trauma. The panic attacks in my forties came as I was working on a book about the accident that severely burned my parents. When I turned forty-two, my children were four and six, the same ages as my sister and me when my parents went down to the cellar to light the pilot light and were engulfed in flames. I was having, what I now know to be, an "anniversary reaction" to the event.

I tried everything to overcome those fears, which seemed to be consuming my body. I drove across the Golden Gate Bridge to see Isabel Gilbert. I thought she would have six cats roaming around a cluttered apartment and wear a long, flowing floral dress. Instead, she was a nurse, very practical, and invited me into her domain to be hypnotized. She talked about the power of hypnosis. "When I moved into assisted living, I was very unhappy. I did self-hypnosis three times a day for four days, and now I'm happy living here." I was amazed by how quickly three-minute self-hypnosis sessions could change her life. A 2016 *New York Times* article, "Is Hypnosis All in Your Head? Brain Scans Suggest Otherwise," shows proof that the brain really does change after hypnosis.[2] Isabel told me that many people tell her they don't have three minutes in their day. "Can you believe that? Not even three minutes in a day!" But there are many opportunities throughout the day to close your eyes for three minutes.

The tape she made for me, now over twenty years ago, has helped me throughout my life. In her soothing voice she says, "If you have worries, write down the worries before you go to sleep and say to yourself that you'll deal with them the next day." She also had me visualize myself happy and confident.

Making lists can also help calm our brains. In the months before retirement, I had endless lists all over the house mixed in with stacks

---

2   Erica Goode, "Is Hypnosis All in Your Head? Brain Scans Suggest Otherwise," July 16, 2016.

of papers to grade—papers that multiplied like rabbits—along with dishes strewn just about everywhere. On top of the papers, I made lists with my financial calculations. My list obsession was off the charts, bordering on disturbed. I'd tear out pieces of paper from old notebooks and write financial calculations on the back of poems or the back of old grocery-shopping lists. The financial calculations seemed to change every day. What was the reality? Sometimes my dog, Penny, would sit on the lists as if guarding them or telling me to stop making all those lists, or get some help! Lists, as long as they are not obsessively long, can be helpful.

There are myriad options around to calm your mind. That's always important to remember as you make the decision to retire. Sometimes making a list can help. I write down some things I can do to make sure I spend less: shop at thrift stores, have potluck meals instead of going out to dinner, use Netflix instead of going to the movies, refinance, downsize, take in students, do after-school tutoring, cut coupons. The list can go on and on and on.

I   I   I

Making lists calms me down; writing down the possibilities for this new post-retirement life relieves my spinning, anxious mind. Neuroscientist Daniel Levitin, PhD, author of *The Organized Mind,* argues that lists help you to be more productive and can help you to feel more at ease.[3] He says most people can hold about four things in their mind at one time. We often have many more than four things roiling around in our addled brains. By putting pen to paper and creating a list, Levitin says you don't have to constantly worry about what you need to do. Lists, he says, take away the need to do "mental juggling." Okay. I've made my lists. But, will this *really* take away my anxiety?

Then the fear surfaces again.

---

3   David Levitin, *The Organized Mind,* 1st edition (New York: Dutton, 2014).

Who knows what expenses will rear their little heads, hairy moles coming up out of the dark soil, in the years to come? Bills seem to go up, not down these days. Many retirees thought they could make it on a fixed income and then couldn't. They refinanced their homes to pay for tuition for their children, emergency medical bills, vacations, or shiny new kitchens and at sixty-five have equity lines along with their first mortgage. The middle-class has begun to disappear in America. When employers stopped providing pensions and 401(k)s became popular, many workers were left with much less than they need, especially after the 2008 stock market meltdown. As a result, people continue to do some work for money well into their seventies or even eighties, if they are still able to work.

I see the word OVERDRAWN written on our backs like the letter "A" in *The Scarlet Letter*.

I hear the voice of Suze Orman in my dreams. "Live below your means!" But, will those means be realistic? Do I need to make a leap of faith?

The night before I go back to school to teach my classes, Jim and I talk.

"We'll manage," Jim says. "We'll get more students to live with us. I'll be happy to cook for them." For years, we've had a steady stream of students from an international school living with us to help with the mortgage and tuition for our daughters. These students come from all over the world, and some of them call us "My American parents." I'm grateful for Jim's solace and his love of cooking. Words from Lewis Carroll spin through my brain:

"The time has come" the Walrus said,

"To talk of many things:

Of shoes—and ships—and sealing-wax—

Of cabbages and kings—

And why the sea is boiling hot—

And whether pigs have wings."

The time has come, I think, to go beyond talking and complaining and act now—to do what I love. The time has come to leave my job. I can feel it in my bones, this potential new life, although the fatigue of working has almost become unbearable.

Pure Exhaustion

Physical and emotional exhaustion set in for some of us when we are on the cusp of retiring. We've made the decision but we have to continue to persist without ceasing. Like a runner pushing through the last mile or a student slogging through final exams, the body begins to rebel. "I was driving to my paycheck," a friend said. All the joy had gone out of her job. The anxiety about money and what to do next can add to the exhaustion. My friend Eleanor, said, "I was so sleep deprived in the last months—relying on sleeping pills and Chinese herbs—that I can hardly remember that time." She talked about everything she had to do to leave her job and the constant worries. Pamela, working as an Episcopal priest with hospice patients eventually experienced compassion fatigue because of the anguish caregiving at such an intense emotional level brought. Many people about to retire know "it's time."

It's January, my first class of the new (and my last) semester. Batmale Hall. Second floor. A long classroom with thirty-one chairs shoved next to each other. Every seat is taken. I write my name and class on the board. Louise Nayer. English 1A. More students lean in the doorway. They're trying to get in. I move toward the door to see how many are trying to register.

"I'll be deported," one whispers to me. "I'll lose all my financial aid," another says. A group of students with more stories stand in the hallway. I'm tired. Bone tired. Can I really take all these students into my class?

My neck suddenly aches; a pain squeezes around my head like a vice. I wish I were home petting my precious dog, Penelope Papillion, aka Penny or The Pooch, her soft, velvety fur so soothing.

I have thirty-one names on my list. They look so eager, wanting me to like them, to help them, to move them through the class. I've always loved being in the classroom. Toward the end of class, I feel a jolt of energy. The students like me. They need me. I'll help them love to write. I'll help them transfer to four-year colleges or certificate programs. But, the excitement wears off quickly as it often does for some of us about to retire. My shoulders slump.

My blood feels like it's being transfused, not in but out of my exhausted body where it might pool on the floor. My cells speak to me every day: "Your walls are crumbling. You need to slow down."

Stop complaining. Soldier on. That voice intrudes like an uninvited guest.

I don't want to die on the serpentine road between the campus buildings.

Then I think of my uncle again. The chance he never had.

I don't think I can make it through another semester.

I put my syllabi back into my knapsack. I quickly look at where I need to be next. The science building, third floor. I have ten minutes to get there. Not an easy task for even someone much younger. I search my purse for aspirin and go to the water fountain to pop the anti-inflammatory pills before I trudge on.

I've often thought of myself as fairly spry. I loved sports as a child—ran as fast as Peter who was the fastest boy in my small class of students—until I turned twelve. Lately, though, I haven't been doing much exercise at all. My body drags behind me as I slog across campus feeling like I've seceded from myself.

Today, I take the elevator up three floors instead of walking. *I've never done that before.* The books I'm carrying feel like lead weights. In a few weeks, I'll be carrying papers to hand back as well, stacks of papers with comments swirling around.

Now it's 2:00 p.m., my first afternoon class in the arts building. I'm sitting down as I take roll. I've never done that on the first day. I get up to teach but feel like the words "help me, help me" are invisibly tattooed on my body, and no one can see how I'm really feeling. I remember the pieces of magical paper we had as children, paper we slipped into water so the words would appear. *Help me. Help me.* These are the words stuck in my throat like tiny bones.

Before retirement, people can feel desperate to leave their jobs. They wonder if their bodies and minds will last for even one more day. Will I die before I get there? Anna, an accountant, had saved well for her retirement but had a mini-stroke several months before she left. Thankfully she recovered, but she remembers the fear. "I didn't want to die at my desk."

Recently, I've suffered from headaches and pains in my chest. I keep going to the doctor to get checked out. Fortunately all the tests, including an endoscopy and a heart test, have been fine. "My intuition told me I had to leave my job," Claire, a nurse practitioner, said. She continued, "All of it is a gamble, staying so long. Some people wait another three years and then get sick." Emily, who worked as a data security and privacy professional, got up at 4:30 a.m. and didn't come home until after 7:00 p.m.; she was gone from home for over twelve hours each day. When she turned sixty-nine, she knew she had to leave. "Why am I doing this?" she said. "I want my life back." It's important that we listen to our bodies. We only have this one!

Can I make it through to the end?

Imagining a New Life

Not all of us know what we're going to do when we retire. For some, the first months or even the first year are ones of exploration. Sometimes doing nothing for a while is an option. We don't all have to fill our calendars with everyday activities; for many retirees, though, this is what helps them ease into their new life.

Years ago, in a different incarnation, I lived for poetry, line breaks and images, and for those tiny worlds that grew bigger on the white page. When I was a new mother—in school and working in the late sixties and seventies and even into the eighties—I always carried around small, black journals that I bought from art supply shops. I wrote in coffee shops in New York City, Buffalo, and San Francisco. Sometimes, when I forgot my black book, I wrote on torn, coffee-stained napkins. I wrote while riding on the subway, at home, and in the middle of the night at "the hour of the wolf."

I've found little phrases in these journals, such as my daughter Sarah saying, "All the cars are parakeets," or "This is the room you've been waiting to inhabit all these years: silent as the thinnest snowfall." Laura, only three years old at the time, once said from the backseat of our white Toyota, her tiny body strapped into her car seat, "Mama. I'm so hungry I could eat infinity!" I have seventeen of those small journals on my shelf at home—whole lifetimes I recorded. I want to write more and teach less.

"Please higher spirit," I say day and night, "first keep my family and friends happy and healthy, and second let me inhabit that world again—channel words and phrases—not grade papers every weekend night, every weekend day. I want to remember the silent, thin snowfalls even as I sit inside a room, letting my fingers dance on the keyboard."

"Calm yourself, Louise," I say in my quietest of voices. Every day when I come home from work in my preretirement-anxiety craze, I pat my fourteen-year-old precious dog, Penny, on her head, massage her back, even hold her little paws: all to help her help me. She's relaxed but looks at me as if she is about to say, "What's up now?" Then she puts her head back down, her furry chin resting on my blue-jeaned thigh. Pets can be wonderful calming machines.

Along with petting Penny, I use a sleep technique I read about in *Redbook* magazine.

Imagine a dresser with many drawers.

Open a drawer.

Put your worry inside and close the drawer. Do it again for another worry.

*Then go back to sleep. You can deal with these
worries in the morning.*

I always imagine the blue dresser with the silver knobs that our daughter Sarah, an incredibly talented artist, restored from a Salvation Army store. It's in our front bathroom. It has six drawers, enough for all my worries, worries that have grown exponentially as I get closer to signing on the dotted line.

It's now 2:00 a.m. on the first day after teaching. I'm still awake. Jim is in a deep sleep. Penny is sleeping, too, on the blue chair next to my side of the bed. I do the dresser-drawer thing: open the drawer in my mind, put the healthcare-daughter worries in there, and close it. But the drawer keeps springing open. For the whole entire night.

I will not worry, I say again, this time louder inside my head. I shove the drawer closed. It stays closed. My daughters will be okay. Why can't we have the single-payer system? Why can't everyone in America get good healthcare? And good pensions? I feel like I could rant for a long time but I stop myself. Why are interest rates for student loans so ridiculously high? The debtor's prison has not really gone away. Many debtors live behind invisible bars.

A couple of hours later, I wake up. Jim is still sleeping soundly.

Another thought plagues me. Why did I opt out of the State Teacher's Retirement System when I was part-time at two schools? My mind is flip-flopping again. Many of us didn't think of the future back then. We were trying to pay the bills, not focused on retirement that seemed light years away. *Carpe Diem*—seize the day. We live in an era where we receive offers of credit cards every day or if you own a home, offers of equity lines "for new kitchens, new bathrooms, or trips across the world." A long time ago, my tax accountant, Julie, says many people would never have thought of having a mortgage in old age. The goal for everyone was to have your house paid off. But, a lot of us have refinanced too much. We just weren't thinking or we desperately needed the money. And for those who rent, rents have skyrocketed, particularly in urban areas. Rents are rarely one quarter of your take-home salary as they were always supposed to be. They are often 50 percent of your salary, leaving little else to live on. Many college graduates move back home.

Suze Orman didn't have her TV show then.

The money will happen, we believed. "Don't worry. Be happy!" I imagine green bills falling in huge clumps from the trees. "The universe will provide." My sister is a life coach in St. Thomas and reminds me of such things. Just relax! Visualize. If you don't see something, you can't make it happen. But I'm not in St. Thomas with the sun easing away my money fears as I sip a mango smoothie and later go for a dip in the perennially warm waters of the Caribbean. What I'm really seeing are bills and not the green stuff you can trade for products. All the bills are going up, up, up. Jennifer Lane, a well-known financial adviser says, "The universe also gave us executive functions to plan." Have I planned well enough?

Okay. I pull out another virtually imagined dresser drawer and put in my money anxiety and close the drawer. It doesn't quite shut. I try to close it two, no three times. I finally slam it hard enough. It doesn't open again. I drift back to sleep. It's now 4:00 a.m. Jim is still sleeping soundly, but who knows what crazy energy he has absorbed from my ruminations. Poor guy. I need to calm down. I'm visualizing my life, post-retirement.

> *I'm at a yoga class, ten pounds thinner. My cholesterol has gone down. A lean, energetic machine. I'm lying on a turquoise sticky mat with my blocks and belt nearby. This is my third class for the week. That's right. I've gone to yoga three times in one week! Downward dog, (which now makes me groan) is starting to get easier since my wrists no longer hurt. My dog, Penny, does a perfect downward and even upward dog each morning and so do I. At night, I do child's pose and waterfall pose to calm me even more deeply into this tranquil life I've chosen.*

> *As I drift into sweet sleep, I also think of how my husband and I can hike more, take walks by the ocean, walk around the new rock-formation labyrinth with a view of the Pacific, or walk on the beach, gaze at seagulls and small*

hordes of sandpipers with their brown and white flecked bodies, floating on the sand like tiny dancers. Everyone is healthy and happy.

Then reality hits. Wham. A wave. I'm drowning. The froth fills my mouth.

Have I planned well enough? Suddenly, this seems important: Who will I be without my job? Will I vanish, disappear, become a little drop on the earth—the "me" who is the professor/colleague, swallowed into the moist soil, nothing left. All these questions zoom in and out of my brain like light snow flurries in the New York City winter when I was growing up in my red brick apartment building on 20th Street and First Avenue, the sidewalk white and slippery. I opened my mouth so the flurries would coat my throat with cold liquid. Sometimes the thoughts come like the lightning bugs of the Long Island summers, small beacons of light hovering over the green summer grass. They are the questions and they are also the answers: the words I want to catch in the middle of the night, the creative life I long for as I near sixty-two years old. My aching neck says, "No more."

When the exhaustion threatens our health, it's time to leave.

Ways to Calm Yourself from Anxiety

Isabel Gilbert, my hypnotist, taught me this simple way of relaxing.

Take a deep breath to the count of four.

Let it out to the count of eight.

She told me to breathe like this whenever I "transition," which is often, from one classroom to the next, then from my class to my car.

We all transition from our car to work or from the subway or bus to work, from work to eating lunch, from our desks to get coffee or tea. Millions of transitions in life, transitions we don't even think are transitions and now become millions of deep breaths. Breathe in deeply to the count of four and let it out to the count of eight. Feel your molecules sigh and then relax. Life is full of transitions, and we can breathe our way through them.

Isabel also taught me a quick three-minute hypnosis, which has gotten me through a lot of trials and tribulations. At the College of San Mateo, thankfully, there was a small room off the bathroom with a couch and a door I could close. When the panic screamed through my system, between classes, I would go to that sacred room, lock the door, lie down on the couch, take a deep breath, and do my three-minute meditation.

Look at a spot on the ceiling or in front of you until your lids feel heavy. Then close your eyes.

Imagine a beautiful place in nature (or a fictional place) and feel you are really there.

Imagine the beautiful smells and sweet sounds. Feel the air on your skin.

Visualize a sky writer, the writing in the shape of clouds. See the number 100 and then see it disappear. See 99 and then see it disappear. Go down to 95 at least.

Then give yourself a suggestion. (Example: I move calmly into this next phase of my life.)

Then open your eyes and come out of the hypnosis.

Of course, your suggestion can be anything you feel you need most at this time of your life. I was having panic attacks while driving, so my suggestion at that time was "I am always calm when I drive."

If you have had particular difficulties from the past, as some of us have had in varying degrees, retirement, or a new phase of life, can trigger old hurts. Leaving your comfort zone can feel especially scary. As part of my tape, Isabel suggested this activity.

Imagine a tranquil scene in nature.

See yourself as a small child, frightened and alone.

Imagine the adult (you) picking up yourself as the small child and hugging her close to your body. You can say, "You are healthy, safe, and loved."

When I remember to do this before bed, it's amazing how refreshed I feel in the morning!

Greet the Day in Peace
Another calming technique that can be practiced daily is a ritual from *How to Bury a Goldfish*, a book I coauthored with Virginia Lang.[4]

Wake up to a Zen chime or some calming music. You can purchase special alarm clocks with sounds of the ocean or sounds of birds.

Put a beautiful photo of someone you love or a calming painting in your direct line of vision.

As you look at the painting or photo, imagine yourself going calmly through your day.

---

4   Virginia Lang, Louise Nayer, *How to Bury A Goldfish: 113 Rituals for Everyday Life* (Emmaus, PA: Rodale, 2000).

FEBRUARY

Fears of Losing a Community

Will I feel isolated and lonely when I retire? What kind of activities might I get involved with post-retirement? How can I find a new community and also keep in touch with my old work life if I choose to? What are ways I can calm myself during this time?

Fears of Isolation and Missing Your Coworkers

"I never realized, until I retired, how much I would miss all the two- to three-minute chats I had throughout the day. That's what I miss most," one of the English Department chairs I worked with mentioned after he retired. Betsy L., retired as an administrator for a newspaper, said she feared when she retired her life would be like it had been during those times when she was unemployed. "My only human contact throughout the day would be with the waitress when I went out for lunch." Many people fear isolation.

I never thought about my department chair's words until the five months before I left. Then I found myself really listening when people talked to me, thinking, *This might be the last time I even see this person.* At work, whether at a huge college, a corporation, or a small company, people say hello or goodbye multiple times during the day. The precious moments are the "Good luck on your surgery," or "I'm so sorry about Fred's illness," or "What wonderful news about the new baby," or "Hang in there" before an employee review. Sometimes I see the same person park her car at the same time, like children's parallel play; just knowing she is arriving at the same time comforts me. I also see one woman, whom I often chat with, always walking her two leaping dogs; another walks a dog that has lost his back legs. With a special contraption, the dog is able to gracefully move up and down the sidewalk and smell the flowers. I will no longer see the dogs or chat with my colleague every day.

My office is on the third floor, lucky for me, away from the fray, but I often go to the fifth floor and purchase coffee for a dollar and have a few moments with the secretary or whoever is passing through. I like being around people, possibly because I grew up in a thirteen-story apartment building in New York City, eight apartments on one floor. As a child, every day I would see the same people coming and going and then at night smell cooking—spaghetti and meatballs, macaroni and cheese, or roast beef—wafting through the hallways. So when I go upstairs, perhaps I'm reliving my childhood: full of familiar people and smells.

Today, a colleague who is a new mother says, "I spent the whole weekend grading and I still have three batches left!" Another teacher and I bemoan the copier that broke down. Sometimes people bring in pastries, and I laugh with a friend, who is also trying to cut out sugar, as we both wolf down a whole gargantuan pastry, not even half of one, from the plate on the conference table as if we were starving to death. I know I will miss these impromptu interactions and watering hole musings—the talks about teaching, life, love, and even death—with those I've known for so many years.

It's reality; coworkers' voices will disappear from your life and those exact voices can never be replaced. However, for some of us there are a few people we will continue to see, those deep friendships we developed. Anna, a retired accountant, says when she went back to work as a retiree, she felt that "people were warm and nice for fifteen minutes, but after that, I become a nuisance. They're too busy." At those visits to her old office, she felt she was no longer part of the community. She did establish some deep friendships, though, and travels in California with one of her former colleagues. When you leave your job, you probably will not see a lot of the people you worked with; however, you can make an effort to stay in touch as you create a new life and new community.

A few months before I retire, whenever I run into people, I hang on to their words as we chat. For the first time, I look, really look, at the places where I've been for so many years. The landscape, the geography of where you work can suddenly become precious, too, because you begin to notice things in a new way.

As I walk up toward the science building to teach a class, purple flowers burst forth on the sides of the stairs. In the dirt nearby, a Big Mac paper box, empty plastic cartons, and class handouts are strewn below, nature and consumer detritus colliding. The wind comes up fiercely on this campus, and I pass the student union and study the mural—dancers of all shapes and skin tones, some wearing feathered headdresses, move to the beat of a bongo drum. In beautiful script, these words dance across the mural: "We have a dream/the dream is alive/Empowered by love/We will survive." I had never taken the time to truly look at the mural or read the words.

I won't miss the concrete buildings. The shape of Batmale Hall, home to the English Department, is almost prison-like, but I will miss the people. My colleague Abdul passes me on the stairs. He's going to the library. "I've enjoyed using your book in my classes. The students love it." He wrote a wonderful literature reader with voices of writers from all over the world.

"Great!" he says as he takes a left to the library. I know I'll see him after I retire.

To get to the science building, I have to climb at least forty steps from the cafeteria. Today, I actually count the steps to help myself make it up the steep incline, using it like a mantra or a prayer. My breathing is labored. I'm beginning to feel tired, too tired to carry on. I pass a beautiful tarnished sundial and catch my breath. For the first time, I look at the words on the top of the dial: *Sic transit gloria mundi* ("Thus passes the glory of the world"). As my muscles ache and my asthma flares up, I don't think of the phrase in all its glory, i.e., we are mere specks of sand in the infinity of time. I think, rather cynically, *My glory is passing.* The words, "old," "elder," "frail," and "over the hill" flash across my mind as I rest. I won't have a new wonderful life. I'll just be old, a shut-in shuffling across the floor in my pink, frayed, fluffy slippers. I won't be able to make friends for life or join clubs or new communities. I'll be withering away.

Those old-age visions that loop and shuffle across our brains can threaten to derail our dreams of retirement. Jacqueline Hornor Plumez wrote the book *The Bitch in Your Head* and says that though the title might shock some people, and of course it's better to not think of "the bitch" in terms of gender, it was the only term that truly got through to some of her patients who constantly tormented themselves with critical thoughts. [5]

Her book is about "how women beat themselves up"; of course, it can apply to men, too. One of the last chapters of her book is called "Old Bitch Spoiling the Golden Years." "When you forget where you put your keys or the plot of the book you read last week, the bitch says, "You've got Alzheimer's!""

---

5   Jacqueline, Hornor Plumez, *The Bitch in Your Head: How to Finally Squash Your Inner Critic* (Lanham: Taylor Trade Publishing, 2015).

Obviously we hope we don't become mentally or physically disabled, but constant worry about aging is unhealthy. None of us wants a retirement focused solely on the fears of getting old. I want to see myself doing new activities, surrounded by people I care about. When the old-age thoughts threaten to derail your dreams, you can take a deep breath to the count of four and release your breath to the count of eight. Getting more oxygen to the brain will help you feel instantly younger.

I check my watch, still a little time before class. My decrepit reveries, after finally breathing deeply, vanish as I take one last look at the sundial. A mythical rooster is carved on one side, crowing in the sun that is beginning to rise from the bottom of the bird's clawed feet. Students rush by the sundial. More steps, and I count again, twenty-three, to a large area between buildings, the American and California flags flapping in the breeze. I stop by a quiet meditative area—a reading room—designed by my friend Leslie and others.

I was at the dedication for the reading area but have never stopped by since. "Conquering the fury of oblivion verse by verse," from the poem "*Cancion de Invierno* (Winter Song)" by Lucha Corpi is lettered into metal. I wonder about oblivion, how we vanish into dust. Then I see the line "Opening/our way/along unfamiliar roads" and feel a moment of fear then exhilaration—new roads, new beginnings. Just like when I had difficulty making the decision to retire, my mind begins to flip-flop. First, I think I'll have a wonderful, active retirement, imagining pictures in magazines of older people with perfect bodies, perfect pearly whites, and always smiling as they swim in a huge pool by a beach with a floating bar. Then, I see myself slumped on the couch, the heat on high for my chilly bones, and the TV blaring, but I don't hear it. Maybe I'm snoring and bits of saliva dribble onto my shirt.

Suddenly, as if on cue, Leslie passes me. "See you at the Trauma and Recovery certificate meeting," she says. She helped me develop the class *Trauma and the Arts* that will go on after I leave. We've known each other for years, first as poets then as teachers at City College.

Our conversations are short; we're both rushing and we both talk fast. With Leslie, I fall back to my New York City intonations, neurons firing faster. In fact, she is one of the people I will continue to see after I leave, but I won't see her as much. We also won't have the work connections and shared meetings. As she walks down the stairs, I see her disappear toward her office or maybe to another classroom. My officemate, Steve, suddenly comes up beside me. He's on a lunch break and walking fast toward the cafeteria. He and his wife just had a son. He pulls out a photo on his smartphone, and I see his beautiful baby, deep set brown eyes, before we say a quick goodbye and I walk up the stairs to my class. Amy, another colleague, passes me. "The children had pajama day at school today," she says, her face lighting up.

"How fun and how convenient," I say, "No need to get dressed. Wish we could have pajama day." I imagine the English Department faculty in dinosaur pajamas and secretly smile at the image. We both laugh, and she goes down the stairs as I go up. Another small chat. The voices come and go.

Here and gone. Poof. Magic is all about that. Sometimes on the BART, the subway system in San Francisco, if a nearby child is upset, I like to place my hands over my eyes and then take them off. I love seeing a smile or hearing giggles. It cheers the mother up, as well, to see her child happy again for a moment.

Here and gone! As little children, that is the way we practice loss, over and over. We cannot really understand where our mother or father goes when they disappear out the door and we wonder if they will come back. "Where did Sarah go; where did Laura go," I said to my daughters years ago when I covered my face. When my hands came off, I would say, "There she is! There she is!" and my babies giggled and giggled. At some point, as we get older, that game is meaningless because we know that people go away: to work, to the store, on a trip. And, hopefully, they come back or at least that is what we expect as the leaving and returning recur.

When we leave a job we've had for many years, we leave the people we have seen every day.

Importance of Truly Saying Goodbye

Before you leave your job, it's important to think about how you want to leave. Not everyone leaves happily with a great pension and healthcare for life. Some people have become disabled; others are laid off; others are angry with colleagues or bosses. Some people walk out the door and never grace the hallowed halls again. Perhaps, in some cases, that is the best way for people to maintain their mental health in the face of an abusive boss, chronic low pay, or grinding physical or mental workloads. However, goodbyes are important, not just for you, but for those you leave behind. If people leave too abruptly, the leave-taking can feel incomplete. Sometimes we need to tell people how much they've meant to us or even talk out old feelings of anger and frustration.

Goodbyes have always been tough for me. I've hugged my children too hard, at times, when I say goodbye. As a child of four, I woke up in the middle of the night, and our babysitter held my sister's hand and carried me in her arms across a dirt road in Wellfleet, Massachusetts. This was our first summer vacation, and it ended tragically. My parents were severely burned in the cellar of our rental cottage in a freak accident and were taken away in an ambulance. The stars, which had been beautiful the night before, dripping with iridescent light, now seemed flat in the sky.

My sister, only six years old, sobbed in our neighbor's basement room full of old mattresses. She called out, "Mommy, Daddy, Mommy, Daddy," all night. I stared up at the ceiling covered with tiny green mold spores and cried on the inside. Everything changed in what felt like a millisecond, with no preparation. My parents disappeared into hospitals for nine months. Children were not allowed into hospitals in the 1950s. My mother had thirty-seven operations on her face and hands and was facially disfigured for the rest of her life. The sadness and the horror were buried inside. When we reunited, we went back to school quickly. Little was discussed. Facades were put up, not that different from when the bomb dropped on Hiroshima and shop owners started their businesses again. The radiated landscape exploded with oleander flowers in a kind of terrible beauty. People carried on. They didn't talk about it. They just carried on.

A lot of people have had terrible losses, and they have experienced how abruptly life can change as well as the repercussions of not saying goodbye. However, even though it is not comparable to a tragedy, before you retire, you can consciously think about how you want to leave people you care about.

By the time you retire, you have been in a long-term relationship with your job with all the ups and downs; perhaps a great boss, a difficult boss, dry periods with no raise, and then suddenly some adulation and money. Burnout has caused you to lift your exhausted arm every morning and press the snooze button on your alarm; you don't even know how you're going to get to the end. You might feel you want to race out the door and never look back. When Claire left the hospital where she was beyond burned out, she had wanted to contact all the families she had worked with over the years, but her mental and physical health were so compromised at the time, she had to leave without saying goodbye. As a single mother of two children, and after her father and stepmother were killed in a plane crash, she fled to Hawaii to find her equilibrium again. Sometimes saying goodbye exactly as you would like doesn't happen.

Some years, you may have felt deeply connected to those you work with through collaborative projects or regular lunches or short chats every day in the coffee room. Other times, you may have felt lonely, unappreciated, and chronically underpaid. A best friend has left or retired—maybe abruptly—and you haven't seen that person again. Some people, like my friend Ken, have been incredibly lucky. "I love my department," he says of the college where he works. "My colleagues are wonderful." He has had a spectacular career and colleagues, which can make it harder to leave.

Ultimately, it is our connections to others that sustain us, which is why it is good to think about how you want to say goodbye. Psychiatrist Ravi Chandra, MD, cites the Grant Study when he talks about life transitions and retirement. "It is the longest longitudinal study of well-being" and followed Harvard alumni for seventy-five years. George Vaillant, MD, who directed the study, summarized the findings, as "Happiness is love! Full stop!"[6] Dr. Chandra, who has worked with countless patients from all walks of life says, "Relationships are far and above the most important route to happiness."

Many work relationships have been sustained over decades. Relationships with coworkers can be extremely important to our mental health. Gretchen Rubin, author of *The Happiness Project*, says, "Having strong relationships makes it far more likely that you take joy in life, but studies show that it also lengthens life, boosts immunity, and cuts the risk of depression."[7]

I once worked part-time as an administrative assistant at a huge hospital for two years. The work felt monotonous, yet I was fortunate to know that at some point, I would go back to graduate school and on to work I might love. But, the connection with my officemate, Nora, lightened my days. From the birth of her children, to her husband's adultery and her anguish, to even talking about the type of toothbrushes we used, hard bristle or soft bristle, our talk every day was like the talk of intimates. We were the only two people in one room for many, many hours. When I left the job, I saw her a few times, but our connection faded. I still remember our precious conversations and how much I liked going to work because I knew she would be there.

At City College where I teach, the offices are constructed of thin, fabricated walls. I remember the faculty members who were but a breath away in the office next to me and the conversations about students, papers to grade, family, and headaches. We passed aspirin back and forth from the small passageway by the heater. We talked about breakups, newborn children, the death of parents. We slipped each other health food bars and overheard phone conversations we probably shouldn't have been privy to. We wondered to each other whether or not we would ever be hired full-time and get tenure.

---

6   George Vaillant, *The Grant Study,* Harvard University, 1939–44.

7   Gretchen Rubin, *The Happiness Project, Or Why I Spent a Year Trying to Sing in the Morning, Clean My Closets, Fight Right, Read More Aristotle, and Generally Have More Fun* (New York: Harper, 2015).

It is this closeness that sustains us. Strangers are no longer strangers because of their shared tasks and their proximity to us each day. People often spend more time with the people they work with than with their own families.

However, when we have finally decided to retire, a lot of us just want out. Our bodies and brains have reached the tipping point. It can be hard to make the effort to say goodbye in a way that will feel good, not just to us, but to the people we leave behind. Randi Gunther, PhD, talks about the importance of the rituals of saying hello and goodbye. Her piece in the *Huffington Post* is focused on personal relationships, but what she discusses could also be applied to a place of work. She says, "As relationships mature, we let these important rituals diminish or lapse entirely." She talks about when we first fall in love, the passion of the hellos and goodbyes. She also talks about the passionate hellos and goodbyes when we greet and say goodbye to a small child.[8]

Letting go of those rituals or leaving abruptly can be difficult. Both my children changed schools in mid-year, a necessary and, ultimately, positive change for each of them at a unique time in their childhood. However, the geography changed. The teachers changed, too abruptly. One daughter had cookies and soda the day she left. The other daughter hardly had a ritual at all. The readjustment was initially hard for both of them and hard for those left behind. I missed the easy chats with other mothers and fathers at pick-up time, people I had seen and known for over nine years. Their friends missed my daughters. "I didn't know she was unhappy," one mother said to me, her daughter upset that her friend had left. "I miss her at school," another boy bemoaned. "I didn't realize she was leaving so soon."

We have all been in situations where goodbyes are too quick—the end of a relationship, divorce, a move, or a death—rushing to get to a person's bedside or longing to tie up loose ends. We often move on, carry on, onward we go, yet something is lost by not honoring the sadness of goodbyes to those people we have known for years.

---

8   Randi Gunther, "How You Say 'Hello and Goodbye'—A Meaningful Way to Evaluate Your Intimate Relationship," *Huffington Post* (May 2013).

Our dear family friend Josee, the blind psychologist and artist from Belgium, attended my poetry class at the senior center and was inspirational in the way she said her final goodbyes when she was dying. How she died was also how she lived: deeply caring for people in her life and always trying to help them. When our children were young, we had rats as pets, one white and one black, Silky and Milky Way, much to my mother-in-law's horror. The long tails terrified her, so we kept the rats in their cages in another room when she lived with us temporarily and when she visited. Josee visited us often and affectionately called my younger daughter, Laura, "my little rat." Using braille tarot cards, she gave my older daughter, Sarah, a confidence-building tarot card reading when she was thirteen. Josee constantly thought of others. As she was dying, her children and close friends surrounded her, and then she called those who were dear to her heart. She saw each person for a few minutes and then told him or her something thoughtful and how much that person had meant to her. One woman, who wanted to meet a man and have a child—something that had eluded her for many years—said Josee told her, "You will meet someone and have a child." Josee seemed to have a magical effect on everyone and, in fact, this woman did fall in love the very next week. Later, she married her new love, and they had a son. Josee wanted to give to others, to leave people with her loving thoughts, even as she was transitioning to death.

A way of countering the abruptness of a goodbye when you leave your job can be to set up lunch dates with people during the last months before you go and take the time to personally say goodbye to those you will miss. Betsy E. did this, and she also bought everyone a present when she left—a stuff bag, a small colorful nylon bag that could fit into a purse or pocket and could be used for carrying all sorts of things. She showed her appreciation through her generosity. One-on-one meetings can give you each time to really say goodbye and to show your gratitude for a relationship that may have lasted over two decades. Smartphones allow us to snap photos with those we're close to before the end-of-year party. Some people might not be able to attend the party, if you have one, for myriad reasons. You can create your own small booklet of photos before you leave and even give them to others as a small gift.

I teach my class and then walk down the steep steps. I stop by the food truck, my oasis in the desert, where I get some coffee and go to the visual arts building where student work is always on display. I often go through the building because I love to look at the student art, but I rarely spend much time observing the artwork. This time, I stare at two drawings of jackets, one in particular of a jean jacket, the wrinkles and the faded denim so realistic. Next to the jacket, my eyes are drawn to a portrait of a beautiful woman, her eyes slightly moist, her hair wild, staring directly at someone, a lover perhaps. I have looked before at the art but not *really* looked. I was always rushing around too much.

I have a few more minutes before I need to get to my office and go to the courtyard between the visual arts and art building. I sit on a concrete ledge, which is always flooded with sunlight, a small streak of light warming this mostly chilly and foggy San Francisco day. I think of how our dog, Penny, spreads her furry body on the wooden floor in our long hallway, right where a tiny slant of light envelops her soft belly. Like Penny, I am trying to capture the sunlight and let it soak into my pores.

When I get to Batmale Hall, I check the mailbox. We share our boxes with two to three other teachers, so it's often overstuffed when I open it. I pull out the mail, and it flies onto the cold, concrete floor, bulletins from the union and a flyer from the horticulture department announcing one of their sales. For years, I've gotten poinsettias at Christmas and bulbs for the backyard. I wonder, *Will I still hear about the flower sales?* When I'm erased from cyberspace, these little things that have given me great pleasure might also be erased. Perhaps, I can call the horticulture department, but will I do that?

I pick up the mail from the floor—most of it not mine—and stuff it back into the mail slot, praying it doesn't go out the other end to the mail room floor. This, I will not miss. In an effort to lighten my spirit, I try to remember, for a minute, the things I won't miss. I smile.

When I get to my office, Steve is just leaving. We share a desk and he is an intelligent, caring, and endlessly thoughtful officemate. We exchange a hi/bye and smiles. This I *will* miss. Years later he tells me, it is still "our office."

Recognizing how much the people you worked with have meant to you is crucial to leave-taking. When my husband, Jim, left his job he said, "I was at the end of my rope." He was burned out, and his lack of empathy made him feel he couldn't offer people what they needed. Yet, he recognized how much he received from the people he worked with, both independent and developmentally disabled seniors. "People made me feel good—not awards or the Commission on Aging." For many years, he returned every Monday to call bingo and kept up his connections with the people there. Monday became his senior center day.

My friend Betsy L., in order to keep up her connections with her job, volunteered to be on the board of directors of her organization. Her expertise and deep understanding of the mission of the newspaper make her an important and indispensible voice as the newspaper continues. Plus, she has a history of social activism and values that her boss shares with her. She can continue to be his sounding board. She has also applied to be a docent in a museum, and she's made some lunch dates with friends. She no longer fears that she'll be isolated.

For some people, however, all their close friendships are formed outside of work. Betsy E. says that when she worked at her government job, she had countless acquaintances but didn't feel comfortable forming deep friendships since this could affect the work she did there. She said she found it hard to critique those she was close to. She has lunches with an old boss and had a wonderful send-off from her job with two of the San Francisco supervisors toasting her and all she has done and continues to do in the community. But, her deep friendships were outside of work. Emily, as well, did not have deep friendships at work. She was clear with her colleagues that she wanted to keep her private life separate from her work life. "No going to ball games with work friends on the weekends," she declared. She knew what she needed and made it clear. Perhaps that made it easier to leave her job.

People are different, of course, in their needs for constant connections. Before he retired, Jim didn't worry about being isolated. "I love the desert and being alone. Don't need to be around other people that much." He's not a joiner, but he does have a few good friends and me, and I am a more social person. "Being in a relationship has always been important to me. I never thought about the clubs I would join after retirement." He can spend long stretches of time alone.

However, some men, in particular, can suffer after retirement. They are often not taught to socialize and can depend on their partner to arrange dinner dates or family get-togethers, or they don't have a partner to depend on. In the *New York Times* article, "The Challenges of Male Friendships" June 27, 2016, author Jane Brody says that socializing, a marker for happiness and longevity, doesn't come naturally to many men.[9] She cites an Australian study that states, "Friendships increased life expectancy by as much as 22 percent." She continues to talk about how male friendships are based on mutual activities. When people retire, the work activities that bonded people together—meetings, teamwork, lunches—disappear. Of course, this is true for women as well.

For both men and women, coffeehouses can be meeting places, the new watering holes. Brody mentions a seventy-year-old man who was "cured of his loneliness" by regular meetings with friends at a cafe. Other people join hiking clubs. Although the first few outings might feel like you're with a group of strangers, over time, these groups become important, even crucial, to our mental health as we navigate life without the structure of a work life. The hiking clubs often have potlucks and end-of-year parties. For our friends Norm and Sky, people in their hiking group have become their dear friends.

However, for some men and women, it takes courage to call someone and say, "I'm feeling lonely," or even "I would love to get together,"

---

9   Jane Brody, "The Challenges of Male Friendships," *New York Times* (June 27, 2016).

but it can also be life changing. Sometimes men, as well as women, have depended on the more social partner to arrange get-togethers; but divorce and death can change the equation. Not everyone has a partner to depend on, or a person becomes a widow or widower. As Brody says in her article, reaching out and learning to be vulnerable is an essential skill to master as we get older. Reaching out to others can be critical when the structure of a job doesn't automatically give people a social scene every day. An old friend in another city is probably feeling the same feelings. It takes one call to reignite the connection.

Reaching out can also be applied to people who are ill. It's a fact that as we get older, there is more of a chance we, or our dear friends and family members, will become disabled. In the book *How to Bury a Goldfish: 113 Rituals for Everyday Life,* my coauthor, Virginia Lang, includes a ritual for "Keeping Faith with a Newly Disabled Friend." When someone is ill, sadly, people often drift away. But if someone is still able to engage with friends, it is important to include your old friend in gatherings. Lang cites a Chinese Proverb, "To have a friend is to love the crows on his roof."

Lang describes how a group of men, though it could be women as well, gathered at the home of a disabled friend each week and took him to lunch. That weekly outing gave him immeasurable joy. As hard as it might be to reach out, it is even more important to reach out to those who need it the most, which becomes another challenge we face during this phase of life. Isolation, especially for older adults who live alone, can lead to higher rates of depression. Learning to get in touch with people, even in very small ways, such as asking a neighbor if he or she needs help, benefits not only the person who is feeling isolated but also the person who initiated the contact.

Reaching out can be particularly hard for those who are shy. Alex Lickerman, MD, writes in *Psychology Today* that overcoming shyness has less to do with self-confidence and more to do with compassion.[10] He talks about how he overcame shyness by focusing on others in

---

10   Alex Lickerman, "How to Overcome Shyness," *Psychology Today* (June 19, 2011).

the room and being truly concerned about them. When he was interested in others, he was no longer feeling embarrassed or self-conscious. We can sometimes be too quick to judge others or feel like an outsider instead of seeing the similarities between our fellow humans and ourselves.

Another difficulty people encounter is when one spouse/partner retires before the other. "Retired Husband Syndrome" is actually a term, which Victoria Lambert discussed in *The Telegraph*.[11] She says that often women complain of more stress and depression when their husbands retire, particularly if the husband expects lunch to be served and gives advice all the time on how to run the household. "You're putting the dishes in the dishwasher wrong," a husband might say to his wife, a wife who has had full reign of the kitchen for years. Monica said she was worried when her husband, Steve, retired. She was accustomed to having the house to herself during the days between teaching yoga and storytelling classes at museums. "I relished the peace and quiet and the option to do what I pleased. It was a bit of a adjustment to come home and find Steve's jacket hanging on the kitchen chair, his papers spread out on the kitchen table, and hear the clicking of computer keys upstairs." She also had a particularly hard time in the kitchen, which had been her realm. However, now, after two years, she has learned to give over some of her control of the kitchen and likes that Steve does more of the cooking. Also, he has found activities out of the house, so they both have time away from each other. Mostly, she says they have gotten closer from being around each other more. "I realize that we don't know what lies ahead in terms of our health, our life expectancy, or what challenges might arise. In light of these unknowns, I find the time we do have together is precious." Not every couple can come to such an enlightened way of being with each other, but certainly having conversations before retirement about expectations can help.

Some couples divorce during this period because they find they want a different life. Hidden problems and resentments are suddenly

---

11   Victoria Lambert, "Retired Husband Syndrome," *The Telegraph*, United Kingdom (August 22, 2014).

revealed. Cathy Severson from *RetireWOW* says, "gray divorce"—divorce after age fifty—has increased to 25 percent from 8 percent in 1990.[12] It's imperative to consciously consider how retirement will affect your relationship. One person might want to continually travel while another does not. Some marriages and partnerships might not make it through this time. However, by talking about expectations before retirement and getting help, if needed, during and after retiring, a relationship has more chance of surviving this huge life transition.

Ways to Find New Communities

Look at the catalog of any community college in your area. They often have inexpensive classes for older adults—ranging from women's literature to theater to history classes to creative writing workshops. You can find intellectual stimulation and, sometimes, lunch dates and walking buddies. Even if you don't find a best friend, the act of getting out, going to a class, and stimulating your mind will help keep you active and engaged in your community.

The women's literature class, taught through City College of San Francisco, now meeting at the Jewish Community Center, has been running for over thirty years. I taught the class for a few semesters and met women who had become close friends twenty to thirty years ago and lived through births, deaths, and illnesses. Some of them are now in their nineties. These women walked together, had each other over for lunch and dinner, went out to plays with each other, and lived for that Monday afternoon class. One woman, Marcia Grant, who sadly passed away at seventy, would read the novels and memoirs, sometimes two times, and take copious notes. She contributed her knowledge every Monday. She never finished college, and this was the place where her great intellect could shine. When I stopped teaching the class and needed to find someone else, I told her that she could teach the class as well as I could, and she

---

12   Cathy Severson, "Retirement Age Baby Boomers Experience High Divorce Rate," *RetireWOW* (May 28, 2016).

smiled though I could tell she really didn't believe me. The women in the class were devastated when she passed away.

State schools and public libraries also have programs for older adults, as well as lectures on any number of topics, including computer literacy, Elizabethan literature, how to avoid being scammed, and tango lessons. Some people join book clubs or go on weekly hikes with groups, such as Sierra Club Seniors. Nature offers a range of health benefits and can be a gentle emotional and spiritual healer.

However, not everyone wants to join clubs or organizations and fill their calendars with endless activities. Sometimes, your body and mind are tired from years of work, and you may need time to transition to this new life. Keeping a journal, painting a room of the house, sorting photographs, taking more walks with friends, or having more alone time are all possibilities. Maybe you just want to be a couch potato for a month or two, and that's all right. You can start small.

Some retirees don't need a lot of new activities because they become involved with children and grandchildren, and this gives them the deep connections and activities they need to sustain themselves. Many baby boomers, in fact, take care of their grandchildren during the week because of financial stress on their children, as well as others in Gen X.

At some point, though, whether it happens before you retire or after you retire, an activity plan is good—even if it's only one thing you will do during the day that gives you great pleasure, something you were not able to do while working. It's exciting to anticipate a trip or a visit from family and friends, but it is important to plan the everyday events. What is one way you can connect with others every day?

Whatever your life circumstances or your needs, e.g., for receiving continued praise for a job well done or your need to serve others and feel connected to the "greater good," it's helpful to do some soul-searching before and right after you retire. What would make you happy? Curling up on your bed and finally reading some of the books you've wanted to read, with no schedule, no structure, no alarm clock? Following a soccer team? Learning how to do a terra-cotta relief through a YouTube video? Volunteering at a local animal shelter? Spending more time with children and grandchildren? Spending time with beloved friends? Camping or hiking? Setting up a regular exercise schedule? Spending more time in nature? Beginning to write your memoir, whether it's for yourself, family, or publication?

Some people who retire search for information about their family history and genealogy and then plan trips to visit their ancestral homes. Others get more involved in activities they've already begun. Barry started doing city tours in San Francisco before he retired from his job as a city planner—wonderful walks in historic neighborhoods showcasing Victorian architecture; the local alleys of Chinatown; the corrupt politics of years past; or the brave workers who risked their lives to build the Golden Gate Bridge. He is planning on adding more tours when he retires. Having a plan to do something he loves helps him move confidently into this new stage. At age sixty-six, Rose Simon, a retired teacher, became a part-time tour guide and lecturer at the Museum of Science and Industry in Chicago. "I just wanted to be with interesting people of all ages," she said. The job helped her pay her rent, "which has gone up at a frightening pace." For the majority of her days at the museum, she guided visitors and some heads of state from all around the world through her post, a World War II German submarine. She also appeared on the David Letterman show after Letterman found out about this extraordinary older woman who inspired so many on her tours of the museum. This part-time job gave her and others immense joy and kept her active and connected to others.

Life is not stagnant, and plans can change as you evolve into your new life. Be open to new adventures and listen to your body and what you need to feel good. Ask for help when you need to. Sometimes people start going to a life coach or search for a therapist. Getting help can be especially important for people who feel depressed and have trouble reaching out. Retirees can become too isolated from other people and activities they love to do. Invite friends over for dinner. Create monthly neighborhood potlucks. Offer to help a disabled neighbor. Whether you read by yourself for a large part of each day or go from activity to activity, you need human connections to feel engaged and alive. We all do; it's part of the human condition.

Ways to Calm Yourself from Isolation Fears

Continue to breathe each time you transition through your day. Take a breath to the count of four and let it out to the count of eight.

Write down a list of people, old friends and current friends, you would like to continue to see after you retire. Reach out and contact a few of them and tell them you would love to set up a weekly/monthly meeting or outings with them or do a regular potluck. If they live far away, you could plan a trip or have them visit. Put a few things on your post-retiree calendar. For those social people, in particular, that can help with the transition. One friend of mine had her appointment book open on a table at her retirement party. People could sign up for dates with her, which many did.

Plan a trip. A low-budget trip could be camping or staying in a motel. Reserve the campsite or room. Or you may want to go on a bigger trip—across the country to see friends or family or to another country. Begin the planning before you retire; either travel with someone or have someone visit, unless you feel you need time alone. Look forward to your adventure.

Visit places in your community—a bookstore, library, or place of worship—and find out what activities they offer. There might also be volunteer opportunities you can sign up for.

Listen to meditation and sleep recordings. Check out different calming sounds that you can put on when you come home from work or before you go to sleep. When your body relaxes, your worries go away. Music and calming voices can work wonders on the mind, body, and soul.

MARCH

Losing My Work Identity

Who will I be without my job? What will it feel like to lose my job identity? How can I try on new identities and activities? How can I still feel appreciated? What are ways I can calm myself during this time?

Sometimes our identity through work defines us and cages us inside a container. If we don't like our job, the container feels hard and suffocating. We want to flee. For those who love their job, the container feels safe, comfortable, even filled with love. This is the prescribed role we have taken on for many years. The walls that at first might have felt unyielding become comforting, what we know, the familiar, the routine—our special office chair; the desk drawer perhaps stuffed with tea bags, loose change, and aspirin; the photo of our precious pet, partner, siblings, children, or grandchildren on the wall we look at every day. Whether or not we love our jobs or even like our jobs, most people gravitate toward comfort and take on one specific identity: the teacher, the doctor, the editor, the accountant, the administrative assistant, the senior center director. Our identity is shaped by what we do day after day.

However, we are complex creatures. In childhood, we are often pegged as the smart one, the creative one, or the mechanical one. I never liked that caging-in—that way of concretely identifying children with their talents—and believed, though, children have special gifts and have limitless abilities to shine in countless ways.

As children, my sister, Annie, and I found dresses and skirts in the wicker hamper my mother kept filled with old clothes and performed *Swan Lake* in the living room, bare feet moving up and down on the rug in amateur arabesques, our faces turned upward toward the sky, our arms turning like windmills until we fell on the ground giggling. We sang in choirs. We did our homework. We ran fast and loved sports. We were fortunate to have so much comfort and opportunities. Life felt limitless. I wanted to be a dancer, a French scholar, a singer, an athlete, and a writer.

But as adults with full-time work and myriad other responsibilities, our worlds shrink. What we loved to do as kids or young adults gets stuffed in cardboard boxes in the basement: piano music, old diaries, tennis racquets, sewing patterns, cookbooks, carpentry tools, paints, paintings. It takes great effort and courage to reclaim what you've loved, but it is possible. For a number of years, Jim and I held "Expression Night" at our house. Friends and neighbors came and did something creative—played a piano piece, read a poem, made food art, or just listened to others. It's a fun and thoughtful way to get people together. While some people are accomplished at what they do, others are just having fun.

Who Am I without My Job?

I'm in the spillover room at City College of San Francisco near the cafeteria, across from Admissions and Records. As usual, I'm grading a stack of papers. Only three months to go until retirement. I put my pen down, momentarily, and think of me: Professor Nayer, Louise Nayer, Mrs. Nayer—the students call me all of these names—and simply Louise in my creative writing classes, which is what I prefer. After all the adulation I've gotten, I wonder how much I will miss *that* "me," the me who moves across these floors, glides through these hallways, or stands in line to get food, anxious to make sure I wolf down enough to carry me through two or three classes. This "me" has raced across these spaces for over twenty-seven years.

In front of me, a group of Chinese students speaks in Mandarin and huddles near a computer. At the table across from me, a solo student eats lunch, his computer open, but he's not working. He's staring into space. People of all backgrounds and nationalities sit in groups, some talking about math and rational numbers, things I never knew about or didn't retain. Out the dusty window to the right, a sculpture lifts out of the ground. I've passed that sculpture for over two decades, abstract cubes, Picasso-like, a person or an animal. I never noticed it much. I pick up my pen, again, but my mind wanders. *One of the last times I'll be in this space, at this table,* I think. I gaze out the window; the top cube of the sculpture looks like a head nodding in appreciation. Who will appreciate me? Who will I be if not the teacher who leads classes?

They've added Ficus bushes in huge ceramic pots to this room, an attempt to bring nature inside. Otherwise, the cafeteria is institutional-drab with long gray tables, though maroon chairs spice up the atmosphere a bit. But like a hospital, I know where I am: a community college. A place with a purpose. And I am part of that purpose, my job to shepherd students on their way to more school and careers. I am part of the institution.

What will it be like, years later, to come back to this very room and be persona non grata, a shriveled up retiree—teeth pulled, maybe dentures on the top, the gray in my hair now turning into a sea of gray like the English Channel in a huge storm, darkness enveloping me. "It looks good, Mom," my daughter, Sarah, says. "It lightens you up."

But I wonder? And with the gray, maybe there will be hairs protruding out of my chin that I've missed pulling because my eyesight is worsening—even though I have a mirror hanging on a small hook in my bathroom that magnifies everything to the tenth degree—dry skin, huge pores, hair loss, and obvious white and gray hairs on my eyebrows. Maybe my brilliant mind (okay, not so brilliant) will get stuck or even grind to a halt. Various aging scenarios run through my brain.

Years ago, I got on the BART train and visited my dad on the skilled nursing floor of his complete care facility. "I'm teaching *Oedipus Rex* by Euripides," I said. In his nearly vegetative state—he had been trying to die, though unsuccessfully, ever since my mother had died a year before—he rose from the bed on his skinny arms. Using his best Ivy League condescending voice he uttered, "*Oedipus Rex* is by Sophocles, not Euripides" and then fell back to his withering plant-like state, possibly muttering, "Stupid, stupid," though I chose not to listen to that. "Oh Dad, of course I knew that. I'm just overtired." I wanted to slink under his bed. I was only in my fifties back then. What stupid errors will I make now?

"Hi, Professor Nayer!" A student breaks my decrepit reverie.

"How's it going, Xia Yu," I say.

"Reading the Kingsolver book for the second time."

"Come see me if you have questions." His face brightens up.

"I'll do that." And later he does see me and earns an A in the class. He wants to transfer to UC Berkeley. Some of my students plan to support their parents in old age. They have a lot of pressure on them, the first generation to go to college with parents who don't speak English well.

I get a tray and load it with scrambled eggs and bacon. High protein meal. I'm about to teach two classes in a row. As I walk down the road back to Batmale Hall, a student from my morning class waves at me from across the road. She'll barely make a C in the class, I hope and pray, at least enough to transfer to the local state school, a great university. Some people get their stride later on.

Another student passes me, a shy young woman. She has long, dark hair pulled back in a ponytail. I raise my hand in a "Hi" gesture, and she smiles and puts her head down. Making contact with a professor feels daunting to some students, scary even. Most of them had parents who never went to college. I am an important person in their lives. If I smile at them, they might have a much better day. I am the expert. I have a graduate degree. I give them assignments. I grade their papers—A, B, C, D. I'm aware of their movements, how they look up or down, fidget in their seats when I hand back their papers. Once, by mistake, I handed the papers back in sequence—the As, the Bs, the Cs, the Ds—and I could feel the energy of the room descend as the grades descended. Excitement. Relief. Disappointment. Shame. Some students thinking, *My parents want me to go to UC, and maybe now I won't get in.* I walk up the stairs to my classroom, feeling a big wave of relief. After May, I won't have to give grades anymore.

But, I do like my position as a faculty member. I worked hard to get this job. Three hundred applicants. Thirty were interviewed. Three chosen. It was my third try after being part-time at two schools for thirteen years. A freeway flyer with my office in the back of my car, no benefits at one college, and my husband worked for a nonprofit. I went on seven grueling interviews at different schools for full-time jobs, and I was desperate for the salary and benefits. I lost count of all the times I had been rejected, and I was so grateful to finally get hired. There were few jobs then at community colleges that are even harder to get today. All I want to do now is leave.

I have a parking sticker with an image from the Diego Rivera mural that is housed in the theater department; a woman in a bathing suit diving into aquamarine water. This sticker gives me access to the faculty lot where I can park, but students can't. I have a special key that lets me into the faculty bathrooms, though, for some reason, I've rarely used it. But it's on my key ring, a reminder that I'm valuable; I'm faculty.

At the bookstore, every semester, I go in and check the shelves. "Have all my books arrived?" I will say to one of the managers. "I'd like to check that my textbooks are in. I'm faculty." The sound of the word "faculty," not an easy word to pronounce, gives me instant gravitas, and someone will immediately take me through the "no entry" zone for the "regular people" into the shelves for English. With 100 faculty members and classes ranging from basic composition to transfer level literature, the shelves go on forever, a wide ocean of English books. The person who would have let me in, because I said "faculty," will take time with me, lead me to my books, and make sure I find them. Sometimes, one of the bookstore workers will recount excitedly, "My cousin took your class and loved it! I need to take English 1A. When are you teaching next semester?" The words will thrill me, as I feel popular like a middle-school girl invited to the best table for lunch. I feel recognized. Appreciated. I'm making a difference in their lives.

However, not all people get adulation from their jobs. Some feel victimized and oppressed by the work or their boss. Some leave because of disability. Hopefully, workers will have something big or small they can take away from their job that makes them feel proud. Steve remembers a meeting when one of the club members where he worked said, "We should listen to Steven at the beginning of every meeting and not wait until the end!" He knew what he said was crucial to keeping the place running smoothly. Because of his great ideas and the way he executed them, he completely turned the club around so it was financially sound with a robust membership. Jim remembers the hugs he received every day from the independent and developmentally disabled seniors. He knew he was adored. Another retiree, Leslie won awards for Project Survive and felt wonderful that young people were learning how to have healthy relationships. Her work changed lives.

However, this role—to feel important and to look for adulation—is not who I really am or even who I want to be. Images of middle school with the constant competition, that constant need to be liked, and the comparisons of who has the coolest clothes are the stuff of nightmares. What is important anyway? Who really measures up?

My parents, with their degrees and awards plastered all over the walls of their apartment, though impressive, seemed too invested in the outer trappings of success. But for them, coming of age during the Great Depression, education afforded them a different life with work they loved and leisure time they enjoyed. My mother grew up in Salvation Army homes and wore hand-me-down clothes. My father's dad became a pharmacist and had a soda fountain. "When he passed the test and became a pharmacist, that was the happiest day of his life. I'd never seen him so happy," my father said. That was a great achievement for him, but he lost the pharmacy and soda fountain during the Depression. My dad's brother died of kidney failure at twenty-four, a terribly tragedy, and both his parents died by the time they were sixty. My father never got to give them a nicer life after they slaved eighteen hours per day to send him to college. That was a deep regret he had, a sadness he always carried inside him.

My parents, who both loved school and learning, moved up in the socioeconomic class and had wonderful lives through education. Their degrees meant the world to them, though we all know in the end it's all about love and kindness. But it's difficult to ignore the tinny voice, rising out of the earth, which says, "You need to feel important. You need adulation every day!" What will it be like when I no longer have that?

Jacqueline Plumez, PhD, points out that some people need applause, adulation, and praise more than others, and that's okay. Socrates said, "Know thyself." That's important, and especially important as you retire. What do you need to make you happy?

Just a few weeks ago, I pulled out some of my parents' degrees from a cardboard box in the basement. My mother died in 2001 and my father in 2003. The frame on my dad's medical degree was cracked, which I replaced, but my mother's graduate degree was intact. I placed them both on a wall in the hallway, along with their photos and my children's degrees. That was what gave my parents great happiness, getting these degrees and finding work they loved. I feel like they're still here, a cheering section from on high. I'm proud of them. My own graduate degree is in the basement, though, stuffed somewhere on a shelf. I never went to my graduations. That was common in the late 60s and early 70s. Many of my friends dropped out of school. Perhaps I'll excavate it from the dust and frame it. It's allowed doors to open. I know that. It's also allowed me to get adulation from my students.

For some people, however, it's not the degrees that have been important to their work lives but rather their expertise in a particular field. A lot of how we learn to do a job doesn't come from school. Mostly, we learn on the job. Degrees are not always necessary, and they continue to be more and more expensive these days. Young people do not want to be saddled with crushing student debt. Many people are taking different routes to find careers and make money. Everyone, however, longs to feel his or her work is important.

As I get nearer to retirement, I wonder how I will live without my students fluttering around me. They will no longer say, "See you tomorrow in class." I won't hear a student from a previous semester tell me, "That book you taught really changed my life. Now I love to read novels! I never read a novel before your class." As I walk out the door and go toward the bookstore, I won't hear "Hi, Professor Nayer," remembering how I used to walk taller, buoyed by my role as professor at this community college where I've worked for so long.

Eleanor, a corporate editor, says, "I got lots of affirmation for three decades: awards, professional contacts, raises, and promotions. I helped others clarify their message and communicate. Whenever I'd get kudos from a colleague or client—sometimes cards or emails, which I saved—I felt as if all my hard work was worth it. As I approached retirement, my biggest fear was losing my professional identity. Who would I be without my work? That question kept me awake at nights. Work had become a refuge for me and signified that I was valued."

Work can often be a merry-go-round with constant things to do. Steve said that at work "Everything revolves around you. You're the go-to person." How do you suddenly get off that merry-go-round and find your way? But, Steve was tired of his role. People can grow tired of the constant movement.

My husband, Jim, was also tired of his role of being needed all the time. He arrived at work before everyone else, opened the doors, started the coffee, and as people entered, tried to make them comfortable. For the whole day he heard, "Jim, the elevator is broken. Jim, the window won't shut." He was the handyman as well as the director. He also planned various activities to keep the seniors happy and fulfilled. At lunchtime, he did a news presentation, which he loved, writing on the bulletin board, picking out the tragic, the comic, and the ironic events in the world. He was an entertainer and adored that role. He also had so many skills that he did everything for everybody and, for years, enjoyed serving others, while creating a family feeling with both the disabled and able-bodied.

His job was like an orchestra conductor of a living, breathing community—making sure others were happy. "If a developmentally disabled person gave me a hug, it made my day." When he shot pool with Slim, Jim, and Peter—all three disabled—Peter once said, "Jim, you're one of us." That was the praise and adulation he received. His personal mission was to belong and serve. He never feared losing his identity. "I know who I am," he said. "I felt lucky to have had the close relationships I did with people. And the program continued. That was what was important to me." He knew when he left he would continue "to be the best possible me; to work on myself physically, mentally, spiritually; and to continue to be accessible to others." He had no great fear of who he would be without his job and he didn't feel a need to plan and structure his future.

For Leslie, having Project Survive continue gives her a wonderful feeling of accomplishment. She is also a writer and will have more time, finally, to write. Her first priority is her family and helping with her grandchildren. She is retired but is going back to teach part-time as her expertise is needed to keep the program running. This program that has helped so many is part of her legacy.

Adulation, at least when I was younger, was something I craved, at times, more than others. My parents didn't believe in or weren't capable of giving me praise, mostly because of their own way of looking at the world. Some of it was generational and inspired by the concept that praise leads to a big head or ego. In the Jewish tradition, as I understand it, the word *kenahora* means to ward off the evil spirit. Don't accentuate your good fortune as it can sound smug or like boasting to others, and perhaps more importantly, you could lose it. Once, at fifteen years old, I played piano on the radio in New York, WNYC. My dad took a small radio to his office on the Upper East Side. When he came home, I rushed to him, almost before he closed the door, his doctor bag in his hand and said, "Did you hear me, Daddy? Did you hear it?"

"Yes, you made a few mistakes in the Brahms." I remember feeling devastated. I had made a couple of mistakes, but most people hadn't even heard that. Perhaps my Jewish father did not want to ever say, "It was perfect. It was wonderful." I seemed to crave adulation and praise, at times, more than others.

"Look at me, Mom. Look at me, Dad. I'm riding without training wheels!" It is natural to need praise. As we get older and wiser, perhaps it's easier to trust that what you've done is important in its own way; your life has had deep meaning and value. You don't crave external adulation as much as you did when you were younger.

For some, however, it's difficult to shed that skin, whatever it is, that defined you for so many years. It is not really you, as we are in the end infinite and can't be defined solely by our work identity. But, we have counted on that identity, held on to it through the seasons of our lives.

Harold Kushner, in the introduction to Viktor Frankl's book *Man's Search for Meaning*, recounts a moment in Arthur Miller's play *Incident at Vichy*.[13] An upper-middle class man is called in front of the Nazi officials who have occupied his town. He has his credentials with him, university degrees, and references from prominent people and shows

---

13   Harold Kushner, Introduction to *Man's Search for Meaning*, Viktor Frankl, (Boston: Beacon Press, 2006).

them to the Nazi occupiers. "Is that everything you have?" The man nods. The Nazi throws it all in the wastebasket and tells him, "Good, now you have nothing."

This man was so identified by his work and his credentials that he becomes emotionally destroyed. Frankl's book leads us to realize that the deeper meaning of life lies underneath the stacks of awards and degrees; however, many of us have found refuge in our work identities. When my husband, Jim, was a student and worked at a Holiday Inn Junior in Circe, Arkansas, he met a man who had recently been an officer in the army. The gentleman was used to being saluted to every day, and his wife loved the adulation of being an officer's wife. Now that he was an ordinary civilian, his wife—especially—had trouble adjusting to her loss of status.

How do we find new identities and feel good about our life after work?

Finding New Identities

As the Amtrak train, the Vermonter, snakes it way through fields exploding with flowers and into the lushness of a New England summer, my sister wonders what it will be like to finally be an apprentice puppeteer at the Bread and Puppet Theater. She created puppet shows for children in Montreal and St. Thomas, where she performed in special education classrooms, and she's always wanted to continue this dream of magical entertainment. The marionettes she inherited from a close friend of the family have been gathering dust for years. But they've always been there, in her house, like a wish, buried but not forgotten. She is now in her sixties, a brave soul as she knows no one at the workshop. Her hands will soon be designing puppets and stages every day. She will live in the world she has longed to be in for so long. She called the other day from Vermont. "I ran away and joined the circus! Dreams do come true. I was picked to be the Light of Day—an important role. I hope I can live up to it! I have a yellow dress and crown."

Many of us never revisit the worlds we have loved and lost. Going back to doing things you loved to do or trying out new hobbies can be both exhilarating and challenging. At fifty years old, my father, who worked full time as a physician, began piano lessons with Mr. Diaz, who taught my sister and me piano over many years. We were both proficient, more than proficient, playing Brahms and Debussy. I played on the radio once and in many concerts. My sister, later, became an organist at a church. My dad, not a natural in terms of his ear, practiced every night. He started with "Three Blind Mice," putting on the metronome to help him keep time. His hands, burned from the explosion in 1954, didn't have the ability to open very far, which frustrated him. "Damn it, damn it," I'd hear him say as he hit the keys. He had to fit his practicing in between my sister and me. He did this for three years and finally made it to the piece "Solfeggietto," which my sister and I played with ease and learned many years before. I remember being curious that my father would practice piano every night and, at times, I was unkind, as teenagers can be, and even felt like laughing while thinking, *Three years and he's only gotten to Solfeggietto!* Now I wish I could go back and hug him and tell him how amazing that after a full day of work, he wanted to learn to play music, to go out of his comfort zone. This is something he was not good at, but he tried every day to get better.

After three years, he stopped playing. "Solfeggietto" was his crowning piece, his glory. Later, when he retired, we tried to encourage him to branch out, to take classes at the New School across the street. He never did take a class, but I'll never forget that effort he put into playing the piano and how he was able to shed his "expert" doctor persona and struggle for three years, plunking the keys, the metronome monotonously keeping time.

As retirees, we have tremendous freedom to choose how we want to spend our time. We can throw ourselves into all kinds of activities and not worry about being the best or succeeding. Author Paul Coelho says, "There is only one thing that makes a dream impossible to achieve; the fear of failure." Hopefully, as we get older, we can get rid of whatever was in the way of trying new things. Becoming a prima ballerina or climbing Everest might not be in the picture, but taking a ballet class or a hike on a nearby mountain are achievable goals. As we grow up, what Peter Pan warns us not to do, we often shed earlier selves: the long distance runner, pushing through aches and pain and getting into the zone; the doodler with multi-colored markers, deftly drawing horses; the cook, the builder, and the guitar maker. Ruth Reichl, an American chef and food writer, says, "One of the secrets to staying young is to always do things you don't know how to do, to keep learning." Recently, I've been playing the piano again. Since I studied for many years, easy and intermediate pieces are not too hard for me. I find that at home or friend's houses, I've been playing pieces I know, over and over again. "That sounds great," Jim or a friend might say. I feel a moment of pride and sit up taller. But, I know I'm not really trying very hard. Just a few nights ago, I looked a piece that was hard. It would challenge my slightly stiff fingers as well as my brain. "This might not sound very good for a very long time," I warned Jim, as I played sharps for flats and cursed a few too many times as I went back to the same part of the piece, over and over. My fingering was atrocious, and I found the "bitch in my head" berating me. But, I pushed through and I'm now determined to play that piece, even if I continue to make plenty of mistakes.

I remember taking a dance class at a local YMCA. A woman who clearly had a left/right problem came regularly, and when she went the wrong way and often used the wrong foot, nobody cared. She got the same amount of exercise as everyone else and formed important friendships in that class. She wasn't going to let her misdirection get in the way.

Senior centers, community colleges, and universities are just some of the places that offer a wide variety of classes for older adults. Many of the classes don't cost a lot of money. Endless possibilities exist.

Shedding your work identity and reclaiming what you loved to do in the past is in many ways taking a leap of faith. The unknown is both scary and exciting.

A Plan

Psychologist Dr. Jacqueline Plumez says it's important to have a plan. The messages that society, especially our youth-oriented society flash all the time, is "you're old and over the hill." If retirees start believing that, then a kind of paralysis can set in. She said she has seen too many retirees spend hours wasted on sinking into the living room chair, drinking, and endlessly watching reruns of Judge Judy. "The vast majority of people don't like change." She talks about lists and planning but not "the tyranny of the list but the structure." She says we need to gently and carefully craft a plan. She also recounts the story of her father who retired early and moved to Florida to play golf, which he loved. But after a couple of years, he had an existential crisis and wanted to get back to consulting, which he found difficult to do. If he had had a plan, a more long-term plan for what he truly needed to be happy, perhaps he would have kept up his consulting and found a more balanced and happier retirement.

Sometimes a plan can begin by asking one question: What gives your life meaning? Frankl, a psychiatrist and holocaust survivor, says, "The meaning of life differs from man to man (woman to woman) day to day, from hour to hour. What matters, there, is not the meaning of life in general but rather the specific meaning of a person's life at a given moment." Everyone is unique.

My friend Dixie, a Montessori teacher, left her job at sixty-four years old to help take care of her grandchildren. Her daughter moved to Oregon and had twin sons, and she needed help. Dixie and her husband sold their house and moved near their daughter. Her role as "Grandma" gives her life meaning, and, in fact, she can use her Montessori lesson plans with her grandchildren. The move, however, was not easy; her husband, in particular, had a hard time saying goodbye to their house in California and mourned the garden he had tended for so many years.

But Dixie knew what she needed. Her children and grandchildren were scattered across three states, and she wasn't near any of them. "You're the only ones who visit much," she bemoaned to Jim and me a few years before her daughter had twins. Here she was in a gorgeous house in Watsonville, redwood trees towering over their long deck where you could gaze out to the water, but she was far away from her children and later her grandchildren. "I never thought I'd leave California," she said to me. The day the moving van arrived, filled with the accumulations of their lives, she and her husband, Jay, slept in one of the kid's old bedrooms, the only room that still had a bed. The next day, she left with her husband and elderly dog, Sparky, up to Oregon. This move has allowed her to do what gives her life meaning: to be near and help out her children and form deep bonds with her grandchildren. Her husband has now embraced the move as well.

For me, the San Francisco Grotto gave me a writing community and inspiration. I knew I would need support, as writers work in isolation. Before I retired, I visited the Grotto, walked through the sacred doors into a sea of offices where writers cranked out novels, plays, and articles every day and met for lunch around the big conference room table. Knowing that I will have this group after I leave City College lightens my spirits. Being an artist is an identity that follows you to the end of your life. The sculptor Henry Moore said, "There's no retirement for an artist; it's your way of living." I have been fortunate to have that identity, which makes the transition to retirement easier, and I know I will continue to do some teaching, too.

For many, helping others gives life meaning. For most of us, in big or small ways, it *is* the meaning of our lives. Jim knew he would volunteer once a week at the senior center after he left his job. He would still see the people he loved. He would shoot a game of pool, call bingo, and then leave without having to fix things. John R. knew he would continue to work as a doctor one day a week. He would not leave his profession entirely. Many people go back to their place of work—whether to work one day a week—or to volunteer. They still want that connection. Others walk out the door never to return. They are ready for a completely new life.

For those who need adulation and praise, it's important to find the right place to volunteer, a community that will embrace you and where you feel you are truly helping. Dr. Plumez talks about the PID (previously important people) who expect to get instant praise and adulation wherever they volunteer after retirement. It's important to realize that volunteering means helping an organization in need and that you have to find the right place where you fit in with the people and where your contribution will be valued. This doesn't always happen instantly. It's a good idea to do some research before retirement and even visit places where you might like to volunteer.

I finish teaching my class, talk to a few students who have questions, erase the board, gather my books, and walk down to my car. I realize my students will continue on in their lives and I have helped them on their way. That identity of helping others, though it can't be plastered on walls, will never go away. It lives inside of me.

Ways to Calm Yourself

Losing your work identity can feel like the end, but it is a beginning of something new. Ways to calm yourself can be to focus on what you will be able to do when you retire, whether it's to not have to set the alarm clock—a BIG plus (at least for me); to have more time with your children or grandchildren; to finally join a book club; to go back to your workplace one day a week; to get a part-time job; to join a walking group; to write your memoir; or to get in shape by going to the local pool.

I listened to meditation tapes at night to calm me down. I also listened often to my hypnosis tape made for me by my hypnotist. The tape starts with "And now you are forty-two years old," and I smile to myself as I'm now going on sixty-two. But it still works. Sometimes, before bed, you can begin by tensing your face and letting go. Then tense your shoulders and let go. Do that for the rest of your body down to your toes. You will certainly feel more relaxed and can then breathe deeply into any areas of your body that are giving you problems.

Another good way to prepare for retirement and calm yourself is to start some of the new activities in the months before retirement, assisting with a smooth transition. My friend Ken, who plans to retire in the next year or two, had never done anything with his college alumni organization, but he is doing volunteer work and giving talks to undergrads to aid them as they navigate the world of art history. He is giving back and connecting with others. When he does retire, this new community will have already embraced him.

For those who are not sure what they want to do, place five ideas into a hat, such as photographer, birder, memoirist, painter, singer. Then pick one for each of the five months before retirement. Explore the possibilities. Is there a singing group nearby you could join? A class on photography at the nearby community college? A memoir teacher? A senior center with artists who teach painting? Get a friend to come with you. Imagine yourself as a child again, open and free to go on adventures.

For many, retirement feels like a tremendous relief of pressure, something you have longed for and dreamed about for months and maybe even years. The semester I retired, I would often go into retirement reveries, seeing myself writing in my favorite cafe or at the Grotto, swimming in my favorite lake in the Sierra Mountains, hiking at nearby Mt. Tamalpais, and that kept me going when my body felt like it was going to collapse.

However, even though I constantly imagined a life free of grading stacks of papers all weekend, terror set in. The void can seem scary, a black hole that will suck you into nothingness. Some definitions of "void" contain the words "useless," "ineffectual," devoid," or "destitute." Perhaps, we imagine ourselves with no money pushing a shopping cart or like Shakespeare's King Lear, stripped of royalty, abandoned by two of his daughters, naked and alone in the middle of a terrible storm. In reality, there are no voids. Something will appear: a stray cat that needs to be cared for, a disabled friend to tend to, a young person looking for tutoring after school, a call from a dear friend who wants to visit and now you have time to really be with her, and maybe a regular practice of exercise, yoga, and reading. For those people who don't have a concrete plan, life will continue in mysterious ways. Nature abhors a vacuum. The poet Hafiz beautifully reminds us of the possibilities in his poem, "Hemispheres."

> *Leave the familiar for a while.*
>
> *Let your senses and bodies stretch out . . .*
>
> *Open up to the roof . . .*
>
> *Change rooms in your mind for a day . . .*
>
> *Greet yourself*
>
> *In your thousand other forms.*

APRIL

Trusting Ourselves and Our Decision to Retire

*How does the past—our parents' lives and our parents'
deaths or the lives and deaths of family and friends—
affect our decision to retire and go toward the life we
want to lead? How does the society we live in reflect the
choices we've made? What do we say to the voices of
doubt about a decision we know in our gut is right for
us? How can we calm ourselves and affirm our choices?*

Although not all people have their actual parents' voices muddying the
water, or perhaps cleansing the water, when making the decision to
retire, many of us have voices from the past that we must sort through
like the mail: throw out the ads and junk mail but keep certain letters
that contain words of wisdom. But whose wisdom is it? What might

have wonderfully worked for our parents and their generation, might not work at all for us. How do you honor the wisdom from the past that keeps you on the right track, while editing out the voices that threaten to derail you from your dreams?

The writer, Anne Lamott, talks about the necessity to silence all the critics as she writes. She talks about these voices as "chatter" that can come from "high maintenance parental units" as well as "lawyers or children." Her solution, which she learned from a hypnotist, was to imagine the voices as mice and drop them into a mason jar and close the lid. Then she begins to write what she calls her "shitty first draft."

Not all of us need to silence these external voices, but for some, deciding to retire can be fraught with conflicting emotions. How do you sort through these voices? John R., a retired physician, said retiring is not always an "intellectual decision." Eleanor says, "At some point you have to let go and just trust."

Whose Decision Is It?

I retired just before sixty-two and still had a mortgage, equity line, and a lot of bills. Perhaps my desire to ask permission to retire from my financially savvy parents who had passed away was to assure myself that my decision to retire early was prudent. But what would my parents say?

I had hit a wall. My neck was becoming more painful each day. I was completely and utterly exhausted at my job. I felt that staying any longer might threaten my health. If not now, when?

Many of us are deeply affected by our parents, older relatives, friends, or guardians. Their choices, sometimes their early deaths, are the voices we live with, voices that live inside us. Pamela said that working with hospice patients helped her figure out how she wanted to live: with more joy and playfulness. Eleanor said that her father was both a professor and an actor. She always saw his dual existence, teaching during the year and acting every summer. He always kept his creative life alive. She wanted to do that, too.

After Eleanor's dad retired at sixty-two, he moved to New York City to pursue acting—until he could act no more. As a writer and a single mother of two daughters, Eleanor had to quell her huge desire to write for many years. She couldn't retire until she was sixty-seven, yet she held on to that dream—held on to it dearly—that some day she could live her life as a writer. Her father kept his dream alive and inspired her to do the same.

Although my husband, Jim, never talked about his father's early death as related to his own retirement at sixty-six, he now sees that his burning desire to stay healthy, is in sharp contrast to his father's untimely death at sixty years old. His father, consumed with grief as the family business collapsed, died from alcoholism. Jim watched powerlessly as his father's liver failed, his skin turned yellow, and he began to lose his mind. The anguish at what happened to his dad is always there.

When Jim began to feel that his job was a burden—like Sisyphus endlessly rolling a stone up the hill, only to have it roll back again and again—he knew in order to stay healthy, he had to leave. He has always been a phenomenal athlete and runs three times a week, rain or shine, which keeps his body and mind healthy.

"I knew I wanted to be healthy into my old age. I wanted to take care of myself." He didn't have to repeat the past. He can continue to be a wonderful father and mentor to his three daughters and grandchildren into old age.

For some, the voice of reason might say, "Stay longer, get a larger pension or social security check," but whose decision is it? Ultimately, it is your decision.

My Story: Visiting My Parents' Urns and Asking Permission to Retire

My own parents loomed large—probably too large—as they were frugal, always lived within their means, and managed to pull themselves into the middle to upper-middle class through education. They also survived terrible, disfiguring burns. They both went back to sterling careers. They seemed bigger than life.

My mother, born in 1911, worked her way through nursing school during the Great Depression and even earned a master's degree, something few women of her generation ever attained.

The late sixties and seventies—when I came of age, along with many other baby boomers—was a period of great experimentation and rebellion with the proverbial sex, drugs, and rock and roll, as well as political activism. There was a consciousness shift for many; working for peace and love felt more important than focusing on money and security. Our parents, who had lived through World War II and the Great Depression, concentrated on living stable lives and providing their children with the security they didn't have.

Cutting coupons, saving for old age by opening retirement accounts, and making sure to put a percentage of your salary toward the future, sounded at the very least, quite "square" to many of us in the 1960s. "Don't trust anyone over thirty" was the mantra. Dylan sang, "The Times They Are A-Changin'." The economy was also doing well. Jobs were easy to get. I flitted from job to job to support myself without any trouble: secretarial work, waitressing, and teaching. Rents were cheap. As a poet for many years, I wanted to be an artist above all else. Also, college and graduate school didn't cost what they do today. The times have certainly changed.

Following in the carpe diem mentality meant we didn't grow old. We danced under the full moon. We roller-skated down steep inclines in parks, jumped out of airplanes (at least my husband tried it), took Zydeco dance classes well into our fifties, sixties, and seventies. We were a generation that would not age.

Baby boomers have continued to be adventurous and endlessly involved with myriad activities. They often take care of themselves in all sorts of ways, and many look younger than their parents did when they hit sixty or seventy. But devolution and the aches and pains of old age, creep up on most of us, even the most practiced yogis.

No one is immortal, at least not in the physical body.

We can't escape creaky necks and joints, loose teeth, torn ligaments, bunions, or diminished eyesight. We can't escape the need for the green stuff to pay for our lives. We also can't escape that some of us desperately want and/or need to retire from our jobs.

Of course not everyone was similarly affected by the 1960s, but it was an explosive time, a cultural shift that affected all aspects of society.

It's just a month before the last day of my job, spring break; I'm in New York City, my place of birth. I've travelled across the country with Jim to see friends and family—my sister, my stepdaughter, son-in-law, and grandkids in Connecticut and, finally, to visit my parents' urns.

Sometimes, I think my parents lived so long—my mother to ninety-one and my dad to ninety-four—so they could keep an eye on me and my sister and our families, to make sure we didn't screw up. So I've decided to visit their urns, to tell them what's up, what's happening in my life now and that I'm thinking of leaving my job, taking my pension and social security early, doing some part-time work and starting my "Louise Nayer, the author" life. What will they say?

They didn't grow up with a lot of money but believed education was the ticket and loved learning and studying. They both went to Columbia University—my dad to medical school and my mother to Teacher's College—and began dating during that time, the beginning of their love affair on the Upper West Side, by Riverside Drive, where their ashes are kept, not far from the Hudson River and beautiful pathways now filled with joggers. They had high expectations for themselves and for my sister and me.

It's amazing, after so many years, how much I want to please my parents. Perhaps we're all wired that way? I remember, very specifically, when my parents were in the audience when I gave readings of my writing. I remember what they were wearing: my mother with her ultra suede skirts that she made herself and her silk blouses, my father with his khaki pants and sports coats. I remember where they sat. I remember what I had for dinner with them on a particular night: lasagna flooded with cheese. I remember what they said or didn't say. The pressure to please them, even though they have passed away, has added to the anxiety of my decision to retire.

I'm not sure my sister and I fulfilled all of their expectations, but I think, and hope, they were happy with our lives by the time they died. Before my mother passed away, she looked around at her family in the hospital room and said, "I created this." Love suddenly trumped status. We told her that she'd meet Farouk, her beloved dog, when she slipped through the tunnel.

In the end, love is all that counts.

Besides being near joggers and huge apartments, the cemetery where my parents' urns reside—inside a huge engraved wall—is near a much poorer section of the city. With the economic downturn, people are suffering enormously from poverty and no healthcare. Many have fallen through the huge cracks in the speckled New York City pavement.

It's a long way from California. This is my first visit where I will actually see their names engraved on the wall. My mother, always organized, told me that when they both died, "You will just need to transport the ashes to New York. That's all." However, at the Neptune Society in Oakland, California, they told me I would need an urn. So I purchased a $400 blue cloisonné urn with birds—even though "the urns were all paid for"—that I was sure my mother would have loved only to find out it wouldn't fit in the wall." I should have listened to my mother. She was so organized. The fear surfaces, again. Perhaps I haven't been organized enough about my retirement decision?

The urn is in a blue velvet cover in our TV room, near the couch. We thought of putting it on Craigslist—with me leaving my job, $400 could come in handy. I'm not sure, though, how many people would buy an urn from Craigslist or eBay? We could never sell it for $400. Maybe $150 at the most. You never know. The urn still sits in the closet, empty of ashes. Maybe it's a reminder that we all die? Maybe it's a reason to retire before I die on a job that has begun to feel terribly oppressive.

As Jim and I enter the Trinity Church Mausoleum, a sign says this is an "active cemetery"; I imagine ghosts coming out of the concrete walls and dancing all night, arms and legs boogieing to the sound of the East River and to the sounds of ambulance sirens. In the morning, they will be swallowed up into their walls again. I forget to bring flowers and feel a moment of guilt and panic when I see beautiful arrangements, some fake and some fresh, strewn near the walls or by the gravesites.

Now years later, even though they've died, it feels like I'm standing in front of them: first apologizing for not bringing flowers and then asking permission like a little girl. Should I or shouldn't I leave my job? What would they say if they could speak from their urns?

I'm not sure my mother is happy that I'm leaving City College of San Francisco at a few months shy of sixty-two years old. Why would I still have my mother's voice in my head? What would she say about my pension? "A few more years for more money. A few years more and you get even more money. You might live to 100. You might need that money. Think about it. Don't make any rash decisions!"

Inflation! Yikes. A loaf of bread might cost $15.00. But I don't eat much bread, and I have a bread maker. The cost of living increase that all retirees have been getting might soon be defunct, on the chopping block. I was counting on that when I made my decision to retire. That was part of what I looked at as I let my fingers dance across one calculator or another, a cost of living raise because of inflation. A lot of people are mad that teachers get pensions. Maybe they will take away our healthcare or our dental plans, and then I'll really regret I got out early. Cities have gone bankrupt and with it the dreams of a pension. Promises made then broken.

"DON'T DO IT." My mother's voice increases in volume. "Don't leave your job, now. Can't you make it another few years? Can't you get some better help for you neck? And why are you spending so much money on chai lattes? Take your lunch to work every day. And, sew some new buttons on your coat. You don't need a new one. That's wasting money!"

Her voice is so loud I begin to wonder if ashes can speak or her molecules have burst through concrete.

I'm wearing a T-shirt and jeans that are old, so some of the hems are shredded. I am sixty-one after all. *You could look more put together.* Her words ring in my head.

My maroon nail polish is half-cracked. I rarely get my nails done. My thoughts drift, *I just haven't gotten this looking-perfect thing.* When I came of age, it was okay to wear jeans and T-shirts. My mother never approved. But, it's my life now. I can't believe I'm still telling my mother that, it's my life. I'm middle-aged and about to retire.

Who cares what I'm wearing? I'm still trying to prove that I've lived up to my parents' expectations.

I look up to their names again. My parents are next to Rita Cooley and Hollis Cooley. Hollis was born in 1899 and died in 1987. Rita was born in 1919 and died in 2006. Maybe they all would have liked each other. Maybe my mother would have gotten together with Rita to play bridge. Hollis and my dad might have talked about the news. Who knew they would end up next to each other—strange urn-fellows. I look at their names again, white lettering on gray stone, their ashes are all that's left of their corporeal bodies.

For a minute, I wish they would jump out of the wall, ready to tell me what to do. My mother was so good at that. I think of the piles of papers on the surfaces of my house. How can I compare? Why can't she just tell me what to do? Yes. No. Maybe.

My tears blur my vision. I really do miss my parents. Their absence is palpable. I can't call them up on the phone anymore, though I try to hear their voices speaking to me.

Mom, Dad (though it's really Mom I'm talking to since my dad has abdicated these sorts of things to my mom), *should I retire next month? I'm about to sign on all kinds of dotted lines.* She doesn't immediately respond. My mind starts reeling.

Mom, I've thought about this, I really have. I still have some savings. We can always rent out our house, if necessary, and live someplace cheaper than San

Francisco. We're so lucky we have that house. Thank you. Thank you again for that down payment years ago after we got evicted—a landlord move in—and that money allowed us to buy a house in San Francisco. We're starting to pay down the mortgage now, bit by bit. But I'm worried, Mom. Should I do this? Should I leave City College?

What if our house is flooded in a freak tsunami? We don't have flood insurance. Or, we find out enormous mutated termites have eaten our house's foundation? What if something I can't even imagine comes up and wipes us out? I suddenly see myself as a homeless, toothless woman at 2:00 a.m. stalking the neighborhood, picking through garbage for plastic bottles and soda cans or walking on the beach with a Geiger counter, hoping for some pennies that will add up to a McDonald's milk shake. My anxiety is taking over.

Calm yourself, Louise. I take a deep breath to the count of four and let it out to the count of eight.

"Plan ahead, always plan ahead," I hear my mother say. I thought when she passed away she would be pure loving energy, a warm glow eternally surrounding my body. I didn't think I'd still hear all the "shoulds" bubbling up through the airwaves, making proclamations from her urn on the wall on the Upper West Side of New York City at the Trinity Church Mausoleum. Whose airwaves are these anyway? I know in my heart she's just trying to take care of me, to look out for me. That's what parents are supposed to do, right?

Mom, we won't have the money for much travel but we have thought about house trades, which would allow us to travel the world. We'll do car trips to Arizona and Yosemite. Not too many trips because the price of gas has skyrocketed.

And Mom, we've decided against long-term care. Just too expensive. We'd be "insurance poor" along with the rest of the country. We have house insurance, life insurance, earthquake insurance, and car insurance. We also have healthcare and dental. That's big!

Are we being stupid, though, not getting long-term care insurance? Will I get Alzheimer's disease and sit in my adult diapers in a rocking chair for five years in a nursing home while our savings vanish and maybe even our home? Everything down the drain, our kids left with nothing. "They can't take away your home," my husband says, and I hope he's right. Julie, my tax accountant, says that most of her clients who have long-term care insurance died before they had to use it. Plus, it's just too expensive for us now.

Breathe deeply to the count of four. Let it out to the count of eight. Calm down, Louise.

My mother's voice pipes up. "I never charged something I couldn't pay back right away."

"This is it," she bellows from her urn. "Once you sign those papers, that will be your pension for *life*." No more paycheck. My retirement will be about half of my salary, which would be enough if Jim and I had paid off our mortgage.

Suddenly, retirement feels more like a prison I can never get out of. I see myself behind bars: the voices of collection agencies transmitted into my cellphone and constant correspondence with big red letters on them—"Final Notice" or "Gone to Collection"—piling up on my dining room table. There are so many final notices that I can't even find my bills in that pile. It's like the huge garbage dump gyre. A gyre of bills swirling around and around.

I'm living in a vortex, a debtor's vortex. "You made your bed; now you can lie in it."

It's my mother's voice again! I can hear her voice through the prison bars. I'm claustrophobic. The bed is too small. I'm cold with just a thin blanket and no sheets. I'm allergic to wool, and there is no dermatologist here. I hate the food. The oatmeal is too mushy with no raisins to sweeten it up, and there is only grape Jell-O for dessert. I like raspberry. I don't even have any friends. Get me out of here. I never thought I'd be behind bars. I don't want to be trapped forever by my decision to retire now.

"Mom," I say, pulling my T-shirt down over my jeans so I look more put-together. "We can rent out rooms to students like we've done for the past ten years."

My thoughts are really percolating now. *Jim likes to cook. He said he'd cook for the students. He's sixty-seven, in great shape, and runs three times a week. You can still be in great shape in your late sixties. He fixes the house when it breaks down.*

"Our house is like a ship," he says. "It needs constant maintenance." Jim just tiled our front bathroom, and he had never done that before. He had a nightmare the night before the big tiling day. He's dyslexic, so he has trouble with left and right. He made patterns like famous seamstresses do to make clothes for the rich and wealthy. It came out perfectly. It looks clean, neat, and professional with small black and white tiles like the ones I love in New York City pizza parlors. He saved us thousands of dollars by doing it himself. DIY, that's the new norm. Just recently, he even fixed our car that had a huge dent in it.

I've thought this out, Mom. I really have. I'm starting to get hungry. I fish in my purse for some almonds and eat four or five of them. But we're going to need to get lunch soon. Jim has been giving me some space as I talk to my parents' urns. He's in another part of the cemetery, looking at some of the "big ones," stars like John Jacob Astor IV who died in the sinking of the Titanic; Ralph Waldo Ellison, author of *The Invisible Man,* which was assigned reading in my high school; and Eliza Jumel, whom we'd never heard of. She was a prostitute and then married Aaron Burr and became the wealthiest woman in America. So many stories.

As I walk away from their urns, I feel better—more like the adult I really am and not a pathetic adult-child still asking my parents for permission to leave my job. I have a lot of people fully supporting me in my decision to retire and I truly believe my parents want me to have this easier life. They've worried about me over the years: full-time work with overloaded classes, raising kids, and driven to write—a recipe for possible early illness or death. I need to slow down.

"Do it," my husband has said to me for many months, seeing the neck and shoulder pain from the grading and the way I tilt to one side. The headaches. "Do it," says my life-coaching sister in the Virgin Islands, who right now is sailing around the Caribbean with her new beau, dipping her body into the blue green sea. She's living on a sailboat and she's almost sixty-four!

My kids don't quite say, "Do it," but they're as supportive as they can be at seeing their mother retire. I think it might make them insecure. We've never had a lot of money or savings, especially when they were young; however, they had enriched lives. They don't want to see me as old. One daughter says, "I hope you'll have enough money." (Subtext: Don't retire if you're going to be broke!) "I will," I say a bit too softly.

"Do it," say so many of my colleagues. "It's time to dedicate your time to writing."

These are the voices encircling me, a band of light, a band of health for my exhausted body.

"Mom," I say as I'm about to leave Trinity Church Mausoleum. "I'm also getting much better at turning out all the lights. I only fill up the bathtub half way. And I know, Mother, in your pure loving energy state, you want this for me too; my neck won't hurt as much. I'll have more time to write and, yes, I've already made plans to do some part-time work.

I think she's still worrying about me up in heaven. Maybe she's even pacing. Or, more likely, she's sitting in an armchair peeking over the side and looking down at my sister and me. Her brow is furrowed some of the time. Other times, she's smiling. She likes that I've paid down the credit card but wonders, why in God's name did I ever run it up so far? Dad is concerned, too, though he's got a bit more of a relaxed attitude about things. He might be watching the birds, trying to figure out what kind they are—perhaps they're different in heaven than on earth. Maybe they have gold wings or silver beaks. He's got a computer up there, I'm sure, plugging into all kinds of interesting research sites.

It's finally time to leave, leave the mausoleum and leave my parents' urns. Their voices will always be with me. Sometimes, when I feel afraid or have trouble sleeping, I imagine both of them hovering over me, my mother pushing my hair away from my forehead, singing, "Go to sleep, my baby," or, perhaps, just saying, "It's time to sleep," in her more stern, practical voice.

Their lives are not my life, though. Neither of them had a burning passion to do something else in their lives beyond their careers; however, they loved to read, go to concerts and plays, travel the world, and see friends. But, they didn't see retiring as a new life. In many ways, they felt sad to leave their work lives behind. For both of them, it was a great loss of identity.

They *were* their careers, endlessly identified with being a nurse-educator and a physician. Also, neither of them had neck problems like mine.

Our lives and our choices are unique. Listen to your own voice and what you need.

Calming Thoughts and Affirmations

Some people retire and never go back to visit their places of work and never see the people they worked with. However, one way to calm yourself before you leave your job is to realize the door is open. You can continue your connections with others if you want to make the effort. Jim volunteers every Monday at the senior center. He runs in Golden Gate Park on Monday morning, goes to the ocean he loves, and then calls Bingo at the senior center. He gets to see everyone at the center and then is happy to leave. Knowing that he would still be there once a week made it much easier for him to leave his job. Jim knew leaving his job was the right thing at the right time. He felt he had no choice, yet he figured out a way to smooth the transition.

I also know I am making the right decision and can figure out how to bring in some money in ways that I enjoy. I still love teaching and can teach memoir classes—especially small classes without tons of papers to grade. I can keep up connections with some people from my work and sometimes meet them for lunch or go to poetry readings at the college.

John R. knew he had made the right choice as well. He had to leave "the war zone." He still practices medicine but only one day a week. He advises people to continue, in some way, the work they loved to do or keep connections with colleagues at work. Emily went through a period where her job was winding down, with fewer hours and consultant work. However, when a key person in her company left, management asked Emily to return full-time. She stayed on out of loyalty, but this lasted only briefly as she became more exhausted and unhappy. She created an end point and finally left, a clean break. She wanted to write and play the piano.

John L. still works on some business projects. My nephew, George, had to leave his job because of persistent back pain. He couldn't continue to work. Although he can no longer physically continue his job, he constantly helps his family with food shopping, picking them up from appointments, and lending an ear whenever anyone has a problem. He also visits his coworkers weekly. Most people I interviewed, even if they faced financial stress, felt confident their decision to retire from a particular job was the right decision.

As you make the decision to retire, it's good to surround yourself with loved ones who cheer you on and can help you see calmly to the other side of retirement. Friends and family can offer suggestions, such as helping with ideas for part-time work or starting a monthly or weekly dinner among neighbors—an often more pleasant way to "go out" for dinner with every one pitching in.

For those who feel lost without their job identity, friends and family can share in alternative activities like hiking, walking, going to movies, visiting museums and libraries, or volunteering at a favorite nonprofit. For many people, retirement means more time with family and more time with friends. Begin to reach out to those who will sustain you through this time. Remember those, like Eleanor did, parents or role models who retired and did what they loved. Hold their successes and happy new lives inside your mind and heart.

There will always be critics, the voices of doubt, the chatter inside you, and the naysayers. Stay strong through it all.

Vision Board and Creative Visualization

What helped me during this time was to make a vision board of what my life could be like post-retirement and then display it prominently on the refrigerator. Some people like to use more visuals; others more words. Search the many websites for "vision board" to check out how to create one. I used poster board (cut to fit on the refrigerator) and looked through a pile of old magazines and some photos to find words and pictures that best represented the life I wanted to create after retirement. Think of categories, such as health, family, friends, vacation spots, and your passions (cooking, writing, or swimming). You can put in photos of grandchildren, family members, close friends, and precious pets, all to remind you that now you have more time for love in your life. It's important to remember as you pick words and photos, that this is what *you* want for *your* life. These are your unique choices.

Sometimes it's fun to create your vision board with friends and/or family and then have lunch or dinner together. Seeing what you want in your life and, more importantly, how you want to feel in your new life can inspire you as well as offer powerful motivation to continue to reach for your dreams. As you open the fridge to get milk for your coffee or the fish out of the freezer for dinner, your unconscious will be quietly reminded—each time that door is opened—that your life will change for the better.

I also found my used copy, with its dog-eared and creased pages, of Shakti Gawain's *Creative Visualization*. When I desperately wanted a full-time teaching job, I remember writing "I am now teaching full-time at . . . ," thirty times a day. She says to write as if something has already happened. Gawain says that we already use creative visualization every day of our lives; the suggestions make it more conscious.

If you are fearful of having to downsize and live a much more frugal life, you can write, "I have enough money to lead a joyful life." You can also find some photos of yourself at places where money is not an issue: a day at the beach, a hike, a birthday dinner with family and friends. Life can feel *richer*, filled with what really matters.

If you are afraid of being lonely and isolated, you can write, "I have a wonderful new community around me." Who knows what groups you might join? What new community will spring up? Your neighbor, whom you hardly know, might end up being your best friend.

Write these phrases up to thirty times each day. You can put them on your mirror as you put on make-up or shave. Creative visualizations can be extremely powerful, especially as we make conscious our unconscious desires.

You have decided to retire—whatever your circumstances. You can acknowledge the past and feel the exhilaration of living in the present and moving into the future with a new life of your creation. Keep those who support you by your side.

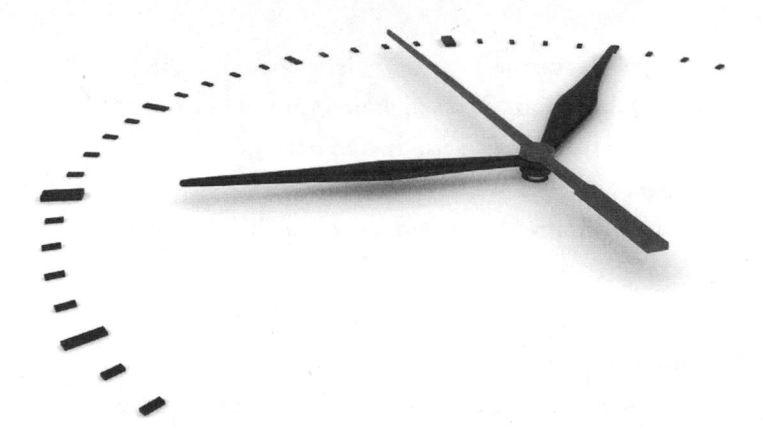

MAY

Final Fears and Finally Leaving

What do I have to do before I leave? How will I handle health fears? How will I hold strong to the vision of a new life? How will I celebrate and relax?

This is it. Fin. The end. Au revoir. Sayonara. Adios. Ciao. Time to leave. The last week of your job.

Finally, my drive to human resources at 33 Gough Street and then the long walk down Market Street to the healthcare system building is over, the internal march to a freedom I have wanted so badly and for so long. At 33 Gough Street, a wonderful woman, Angie, clearly explains everything and gives me a special signing pen to keep. I take the pen graciously. Twenty-seven pages of signatures. "Resign and retire" is the box I checked. I remembered how much—how desperately—I wanted a full-time job, now eons ago.

After I get my packet, I walk to the health services system building, only four blocks away. Making sure Jim is included on my healthcare is complicated. This is my third visit. I've also had to drop my daughter, Laura, from my coverage. That signature was hard to do. We just can't afford to keep her on the plan any longer. Not everyone has to sign so much, but for everyone, whether getting Medicare or Social Security benefits, the paperwork can be daunting.

I'm fortunate that Jim has been with me through all of it. I'm still standing. And, I haven't died yet. I hope I can still have that healthy life that awaits me. Except for some last minute recalculations of my service credit, the years I'll get for my pension, everything is dotted, signed, sealed, and just about delivered.

Some of us have bought houses and signed on many dotted lines. We've rented apartments, bought cars. But this signing feels different—final. You can't sell it back, move, or refinance. You won't get a new retirement like you can get a new car. For many, that final signing feels like an enormous relief. One of my friends, though, said, "My hand was shaking."

Sometimes, it's good to bring an advocate along to the signing, another pair of eyes for such an important event, similar to people bringing friends or family with them to their doctor's appointments. From Social Security payments to living off investments, making sure we get all our "years" can be fraught with fears. For those who will be living off investments, they might want to be more conservative—a fixed interest rate for more long-term security. Big decisions. Sometimes numerous phone calls can be annoying, aggravating, and cause splitting headaches. Often we're placed on hold as the ubiquitous Muzak plays on a loop in the background. These phone calls go on forever.

I tried a last gasp attempt to add to my service credit, thinking my two pregnancies might be time I could buy back. But pregnancy as a disability was not a law in 1984 and 1986. Five calls were made back and forth to the College of San Mateo. The woman who said, "Sorry. You can't buy back that time," was sincerely sorry.

Some people I talked to at the State Teacher's Retirement System, at the Social Security Administration, and at City College were true heroes, shepherding me, and many others, through what can be a demoralizing experience. Others were abrupt and didn't answer my questions. One time, I hung up the phone and cried. The roller-coaster ride of emotions can make a simple phone call exhausting, even punishing, during this time. All of us feel irritated and aggravated by these financial phone calls. It's important to persist, though, to make sure everything is in order.

When I get home from the day of signings, I immediately pet my dog, Penny. What would she say about signings? "Humans are a strange breed. Just pet me, feed me, walk me, and love me. That's all."

I'll be able to spend more time at home with her now, a huge perk of retiring.

Cleaning Your Workspace

The act of cleaning out your workspace is similar to finally cleaning out your garage: what to toss, what to keep, examining your work life while rifling through stacks of papers and faded to-do lists. Suddenly, the time is now and squarely in front of you. You have no choice but to get rid of things. For some of us, we actually spend more waking hours at our offices than we do at home. The smells of coffee, pastries, and lunches, the sounds of our coworkers, or for teachers, the sounds of students coming in and out—these are the sounds we have lived with for twenty, thirty, or forty years. My friend Betsy E., retired from working with a homeless program in San Francisco. She remembers the act of organizing everything, making sure she left policies, procedures, and other important components of her daily tasks in good shape. She organized spreadsheets and databases to input information for her work with nonprofits and to figure out if she and her husband could actually retire. She had an easy retirement. "I was prepared and got the office prepared for the next person," she said.

For Jim, cleaning out his office meant sorting through many photographs of family and clients, presents, ceramic pieces, paintings, and drawings that had been given to him over many years. These were precious treasures to him. How could he throw them out? For him, so many of the people, many whom had died, were part of his heart and soul. What do you keep and what do you throw out? He couldn't part with many of the photographs. Some are on his wall in his art room, and some are in boxes in the garage. Uncle Bill's artwork hangs all over our house.

My friend Dixie carted home boxes and boxes of creative lesson plans she had used with the children over the years. She left some of the lessons at the school and will use some of them with her grandchildren, but she's not sure what to do with the rest. They might end up in the dumpster. Many of us at the end of a job we held for a long time are also anxious to suddenly get rid of things. It's hard to find people who want to take all your work and store it someplace else.

Leslie, a retired community college instructor and head of Project Survive, had the ability to clean her office slowly and says that's a good way to go. She would take a couple of boxes home each week and immediately deal with them—toss or save and put away. It was not so overwhelming that way. She also passed on a wonderful art deco poster of the fiftieth anniversary of City College to the archives at the library. Pieces of her office live for posterity.

For many of us, as we clean out our offices, we're aware of leaving a legacy as I did when I passed on some of my assignments to my officemate. Barry, a retired City Planner, is a firm believer in "succession planning." He wants to make sure that the next person will have an easy transition to the job. He talks about brain dump, sharing what he's learned over his work life and generously offering everything he knows about the job to the next person in line.

The pieces of our work lives that go to others help make their work-life journeys a bit easier. The other pieces of our work lives that hide in boxes in garages and attics or find a comfortable place in our living rooms or dens help keep what we loved from the past as part of our new life.

It's the last week of the last month of my time at my job. I'm doing one of the final cleanings of my office. I'm wearing a pink and white scarf over my nose and mouth so my asthma won't kick up. I look like a bank robber or some other sort of villainous criminal! At the bottom of a huge drawer—with papers I haven't looked at for well over a decade—I find the small dark pellets of mouse droppings. Will I get the hantavirus?

Hantavirus is a life-threatening disease spread to humans by rodents that has symptoms similar to influenza. I did a quick wiki check. *Life-threatening.*

People die of all kinds of strange things. Once, when I was pregnant with Sarah and Jim was away for the day, I needed wite-out and mixed some old Wite-Out with another liquid that was supposed to make the clumpy Wite-Out less clumpy. I felt like a chemist. I was in our poorly ventilated bathroom on Spruce Street. I immediately felt dizzy, had trouble breathing, and called poison control, which assured me I should be fine and told me to drink a lot of water. "Call back if you're still having trouble breathing." The bottle said, "Fumes can be fatal," something I noticed in black print after I mixed the two bottles. I guzzled water. I put my hand over my belly, hoping my baby was moving. "DEAD FROM WITE-OUT" the headlines would read. Like a Perry Mason or CSI investigation, no one would have figured out how a healthy, pregnant woman could have suddenly died on her bed. Then a swift investigator, or perhaps my poor husband, would find the bottle of Wite-Out in the bathroom. The culprit, the poison, indeed, the murder weapon!

Now, death could sneak up on me from the hantavirus. I immediately think, *AND I DIDN'T EVEN GET TO RETIRE!* Take a deep breath. "Everything is okay," I say to myself. Before today's discovery, I did hear there were mice in our offices and cleaned all the surfaces with Lysol, stopped bringing in food to the office as I tend to eat about eight times a day, and I washed my hands a lot and for a long time, making sure I got soap between all of my fingers.

I rush to the bathroom, wash my hands, and get some paper towels, which I wet slightly to capture the rest of the pellets. I forget that I have the scarf wrapped around my face and get some strange stares in the hallway. I apologize to my mother, again, for not cleaning up as much as she did, and I hear her voice, "How could you not have cleaned that drawer for so many years?! And with mice in the office?"

I'm pulling out all the files and I see my community college credential; FOR LIFE: LANGUAGE ARTS is emblazoned across the top. I wonder how long my life will be? I keep my credential, of course, though I've made a commitment to try for at least a year to set up workshops at my house and not apply to teach a class at City College again, as tempting as it will be financially. I am going to finally have my "salon" at my house, serving tea and coffee and mentoring young and new writers. With severe budget cuts, there won't be any jobs anyway for retirees. Many older people are no longer retiring. The ones who do often find they don't have enough money and compete for jobs at grocery stores, retail outlets, or doctors' offices. So many young people need work as well. But who knows what the future will bring? "There are many options out there. There are many options out there." A mantra I repeat to myself.

I continue to clean up the mouse pellets, then wash my hands again and go back to moving through old files. In one file, I see an article I wrote in 1987 about my friend Laura Schaffer, who died of AIDS— one of the first women to die of the disease in the AIDS ward at San Francisco General Hospital. I remember how terribly thin she got, her halting walk to the bathroom with her IV pole a steady companion. Between her many hospitalizations, she was home. Jim would stop by her house on his way to work and make her thick protein shakes. We saw her often during her dying days. I think about her and her bright, kind blue eyes. She had just met the love of her life—a musician and carpenter named Michael. He was with her until the end, even joking with her as he picked out T-shirts for her to wear. "Pick a different one," she said from her bed, a booming voice for her eighty-pound body. I don't want to wear red today!"

"Okay, dear, you're the boss," he would say. She was very particular.

Laura died about a year after she was diagnosed. She never got to marry Michael, never got to work until retirement, never got to have a life past forty-one. She bravely got herself out of bed for her fortieth birthday party. I remember she wore a paisley shirt and her kind blue eyes looked as if they were lighthouses, already searching for another realm where she would rest.

When Jim runs every week in Golden Gate Park, he thinks of all the people who have passed on—and there have been many—young and old, including Laura Schaffer, their gentle spirits floating among the trees and grass.

I'll keep the article—*Living Her Dying*. Who knows? Maybe I can rework it since I never completed it or sent it out for publication. I'll have the time now. Not only do I get to live past forty but I get to live past retirement, too.

Over the last few months, I've known people who died. One friend has metastatic cancer. She has been posting pictures of herself on Facebook—from a beautiful wide-eyed child in Ireland to her now still beautiful thinning visage with a huge head of curly white hair and an endearing smile. The last picture I saw was on Mother's Day with her daughter, both with their cheeks touching, her daughter's eyes, sad and a bit terrified. After all, it is a mother who first tethers you to this earth.

We don't really know what the finish line of our lives will be. All kinds of lumps begin to appear as we age. Penny, now fifteen, has big lumps on her ears. "Just part of the aging process," the vet says, feeling them to make sure they're moveable. We really don't want her to have surgery at this age. But, these lumps and bumps can be scary.

"Though I was in excellent health," Jim said, "thoughts of a heart attack, stroke, or a fatal accident haunted my final days of work. It didn't help to acknowledge those fears as irrational. What mattered most was that after fifty-four years of paying into Social Security, I was going to be stopped short of the finish line. Woe to the wage slave who doesn't receive his or her pittance."

I have another hour until I need to leave for home, so I continue making piles: recycling, maybe keep, and keep. I'm trying to get as much done as possible. My officemate, Steve, happily got a full-time job, which he truly deserved. He is extremely neat and has even cleaned the windows twice since we've been sharing an office, standing on a chair outside with his sponge full of Windex. Now, we both can clearly see the grass and trees out the window. A cubicle with a view. I want to leave the office in good shape, pass the torch minus the mouse droppings. He has also graciously taken some of my lesson plans. I couldn't bear to part with all of them. "I can use them," he says eagerly. My nervous system relaxes. My lesson plans will go on.

One voice says, *Just get rid of everything. Throw it out!* But I want to be careful about that. I remember being told my black toe shoes were whisked away into some bag for charity when my parents moved from New York City to California. I worked hard to get on toe (if only for a year) and I wanted to hang them from the wall, the black ribbons streaming down—an emblem of Saturday mornings at Madame Tarasova's ballet school in New York City. My friend Nancy, now sadly passed away from ovarian cancer, and I used to go and rub our stomachs and smile when Madame Tarasova wasn't looking, all in anticipation of going to Chock full o' Nuts afterward and getting a hot dog and lemon meringue pie. Therefore, I need to be careful about throwing away absolutely everything collected from this life I've led for so many years.

But how do we decide what to throw out and what to keep? We don't want boxes and boxes of paper just gathering dust in our homes.

As we go through the boxes, a rush of feelings surface: pride at what we've done and some sadness at the disappointments along the way. Jim believed the program he started, integrating developmentally disabled seniors with independent seniors would be a model for centers around the country. "That didn't happen," he said. "Perhaps I was naïve in thinking it would." He did start an alcohol treatment program in the Tenderloin section of San Francisco that still exists. He feels great pride in that. He also directed a radio show on KALW for two years, "San Francisco Surreal Journal," but his favorite job was as director of the North of Market Senior Center. Thirty years later, he still gets together with the people he worked with.

Betsy E. talks about not getting promotions she knows she deserved. Politics is always at play in jobs and can cause great disappointments. Yet, she felt gratified and happy with the great work she did and now continues to do in her community. Barry said, "I didn't achieve everything because I was not so into the politics. But I'm proud of my contribution."

As I looked at my evaluations, I recognized that I always got graded down for organization. Perhaps I could have worked harder at that. I don't think, though, that's what will be on my epitaph: *She could have been more organized*. Maybe it's a brain thing or rebellion against my mother who always had all her ducks in a row? It doesn't really matter. I seem to find most everything I'm looking for—eventually.

Most retirees are computer literate, and while some of us may not know a lot about Facebook or social media in general, the computer has allowed us to email long-lost friends and keep in touch with those we love. As a writer, the computer has made my life incredibly easy; no longer do I need to retype whole pages or use the dreaded Wite-Out. For many, their job depends on their computer skills. For some retirees, though, computer programs created to make life more organized can feel daunting. I thought I'd teach online classes after I retired; however, when I started to go through the training, I decided it wasn't for me. I didn't want to invest the time in learning this new skill. Plus, I like face-to-face interaction and I know I'll need more of that when I retire. With the new healthcare mandates, John R. said he felt the need to constantly input data in a computer gave him less time with patients. On the other hand, computers help retirees find part-time jobs, do endless research, provide mental agility exercises, and connect people around the world, which can be an important lifeline, especially if you live alone.

Focusing on goals you've achieved, the friends you've made, and the time and good, hard work you've invested in your job are what you want to embrace and what remains crucial at the end. John R. said when he told his patients he was retiring, even the grumpiest patient who never seemed happy, fought back tears. Jim said he was beyond touched, and he was almost embarrassed at his end-of-the-year party. He received so many gifts and countless people came to hug him with tears in their eyes.

What kind of legacy do we leave as we retire? Erik Erikson, famous psychoanalyst who wrote about the life stages, talks about the last stage of life as "integrity vs. despair." If we've felt good about what we've done and we're leaving a legacy, we can move into this last stage more easily and not succumb to depression.

Betsy E., who worked with seniors for many years and with a homeless program, was proud to have everything organized for the next person who would take over her job. Leslie, who ran Project Survive at City College, which trains peer educators to visit classrooms and educate students on healthy relationships—spent many hours creating an instructional manual with step-by-step procedures to follow so that the job responsibilities and tasks were clear. She wanted to ensure everything related to her job was in order as she passed the torch.

When I see my class lists, thousands of students I've taught over the years, a sob catches in my throat for this is the legacy I've left. Some never graduated, some went on to four-year colleges and universities, to graduate schools and professional schools. Some have become my friends. For me, these are the torches, the lights I've sent out into the world. But, I can't keep the grade sheets. I need to toss them out.

Those names, dots and lines, will be recycled, though I hope not into a huge garbage dump, the mile-long gyre in the middle of the ocean. I do keep the personal cards from colleagues and students.

As I continue my office cleaning, I find the plan for a workshop my friend Leslie and I did for "flex" day, "From Part-Time to Full-Time"—a class we set up for our part-time colleagues to help them get full-time jobs. We were both part-time for too many years.

I interviewed many times, studying for hours, preparing a lesson plan, writing a timed essay, answering numerous questions given to me the day of the interview, taped to a huge podium, as committees of five or six took notes each time I gave an answer and rarely looked up. It was daunting.

"You have to dress up and pretend they know nothing about you even though you've been part-time for years. You have to tell them everything—as if you've just stepped off a plane from the East Coast. You have to study what they're looking for." I remember how Sarah and her godmother, Ginny, went to Macy's petite department (without me)—where I had never shopped even though I'm short—a week before my interview and bought me a turquoise silk suit that fit perfectly. "You got the job because of the suit," friends teased.

I actually never worked harder in my life than trying to get that job— to compete with so many for the prize. I take a deep breath. This job I worked so hard to get is really and finally coming to an end.

For many of us, as we clean our offices, we think back to that person, who years ago, so desperately wanted or needed this job. Now, some of us desperately want and need to leave the job.

"At least the job will end before I end," I whisper to myself. "I'm grateful for that."

As I clean, I look out at the tree I've admired, year after year, from my office window. "Goodbye tree," I say and then begin to say goodbye in my mind to everything on this campus: the mailbox on Phelan Avenue where I mailed Valentine cards to my grandchildren in Connecticut, college applications for my daughters, bills, thank-you notes, and manuscripts, hoping against hope that my memoir would get published. I mailed applications to Camp Mather, our magical summer place. Sometimes I even kissed an envelope before I put it the slot. "Goodbye mailbox." This mailbox knows so much and says so little. Goodbye office, goodbye fifth floor coffee, and goodbye classrooms—so many of them over twenty-five years filled with so many eager faces.

What some people find exceptionally hard is leaving the routine of life, walking down the same path every day, talking to the same people. Where will I fit in? For others, this leaving is exhilarating while others say, "Good riddance." They've had enough.

For most of us, our emotions go up and down the roller-coaster ride of retiring.

Fears of Death or Getting Sick

As I leave and get closer to the finish line, the fears surface as if rising like a huge, angry fish out of the sea, *Who do you think you are? You're not going to do this? You'll get sick or die. Just see!* **Sad news to report. Sad news to report**. I toss and turn at night, trying to quell their loud voices, sometimes resorting to the blue Tylenol PM pills though I apologize to my liver before I take one. *How do you get to do this while other people don't?* There are those voices again. Suddenly, I have survivor's guilt. *Why do you deserve this?* My inner voice scolds me. Will I get sick before I get there? Will my body finally relax into some disease state that was lying in wait for years? *Ha, ha, ha! You don't get to retire,* my body will be mocking.

In the last months before he retired, Jim woke up sweating in the middle of the night from dreams that he was going to die. Before John L. left his high-powered business job, he worried about his health because of all the global travel and his twenty-four/seven lifestyle. He would go to remote locations in China where the air pollution was high. He also worried that flying so much was compromising his health. John R., retired as a doctor, said he wasn't really taking care of himself. He finally got glasses with a new prescription *after* he retired. Other people truly have had life-threatening illnesses, cancer and heart attacks, and hope and pray their heart stays strong and the cancer is in remission, so they can enjoy this last phase of their life.

I try to act stronger than these dark voices attempting to bring me down. I visualize, again, my post-City College teaching life and relax my cells and immune system. *I can do this. I will do this. I need to do this. I've figured out a way to do this.* I repeat these lines like a mantra throughout the day, as I clean my office, making sure to take a deep breath to the count of four and let it out to the count of eight. I put stacks of papers I need to go through on the shelf under the window. I grab my coffee cup, throw away my orange peels, and pick up my purple lunch box. I shut the door.

Now it's time to go food shopping.

Jim and I often go to the Diamond Heights Shopping Center in San Francisco, just up the hill from where we live on Bosworth Street. The center is mainly one big parking lot, and there are always parking places. If I go there more than once a day, I might spend five minutes looking for my car, a silver 2003 Toyota, among other silver Toyotas. Will my retiree brain make it even harder to find my car? The only distinguishing features are that one of the tires has no hubcap since it was stolen and never replaced and I have my children's college, Oberlin, in gold letters, though now fading, on the back windshield. Thank god for that name, especially in crowded movie theater parking lots where I might be walking up and down, looking, and calling out my car's name, "Stella Luna, where are you?" For a minute, I imagine myself eternally looking for my car as if by leaving my job I can no longer be in the driver's seat.

Today, only a couple of weeks before I'm retiring, I buy broccoli, onions, garlic, chicken breasts, milk, and Oregon Chai—a recently developed sugary addiction—and leave the store with my one shopping bag. I drive on O'Shaughnessey, a long and windy hill heading down to my house. I stop at the first stop sign by St. Aidan's Church where I hope to go every Saturday and do yoga for my new healthy body. I instinctively, for some reason, feel below my left ear. Sometimes I twirl my hair, almost pick my nose, and hope no one is watching. Suddenly, even though there are other cars behind me, I can hardly move. The skin is a bit dry, my fingers a bit moist, but that's not a shocker. I feel a lump. It's hard. It doesn't move like a cyst. It doesn't move at all.

I knew cancer might come like this, a stranger in the night, a thief in the dark. It would have been growing for five, ten years; perhaps starting after I stepped in front of a huge power line or nuclear radioactive waste blew from somewhere far away or pesticides started buying apartments in my neck. And because of my neck problems, I've been over-radiated in that area. Once, I even asked the doctor hired by my workplace, who was trying to prove I didn't have neck pain, to use the X-rays that were just taken three months before. He refused. "No," he said. "I need to take my own."

So it's his fault, I'm thinking now as I feel the lump, the *hard* lump. That extra radiation pushed my dividing cells over the edge and a rogue one was formed. I also stopped taking my Vitamin C, which I heard strengthens the cells walls. This is it; and the lump is so near to my brain. I have a moment of getting teary-eyed. My children are grown but not totally grown. Who wants to lose a mother in her twenties? My mother was around until I was in my fifties. Hearing your mother's voice, a lot of the time, can be soothing, bring you back to being cradled and loved unconditionally. They'll lose that. They're still sowing their wild oats. They need me—okay, not a lot and sometimes I call them too much—but more than I think at times. At least they want to know I'm here. I think of my husband, getting up without me, going to sleep without me. I can see him crying. Maybe he wouldn't be crying in the morning when I talk to him too much and he's not awake, and, of course, he can watch sports in any room and not worry about bothering me, but other times during the day he'll be crying. He's making a sculpture of my head. Maybe he'll even talk to that head when I'm gone.

And then there's the sickness and illness part. I'm not sure I even want my children around me to see me getting thinner and thinner; that would be too hard on them. If I'm going to die, I want to do it quickly. Maybe I need to begin to say my goodbyes now. I need to write some things down—what I want to pass on to my girls, my baby, grown-up girls. Maybe I should make a tape, so they can listen to my voice telling them wise things about life; I'll always love them even when I die; and they'll always have my love with them to keep them strong. I'll be a constellation in the sky, always protecting and loving them.

"I'll never really leave you," I want to shout. "I'll always be there for you. Forever and ever!"

I let my pointer finger run over and over the lump behind my ear. I drive down the hill, as I have no choice since a car is behind me. I think of pulling over to get myself a bit more together before I go home to Jim and my dog Penelope Papillion Patten-Nayer, as I've started calling her in a singsong voice many times during the day

I'm already thinking of refusing chemo, even though I'm just sixty-one. That's something people do in their eighties, refuse chemo. But I don't want poison coursing through my system. At least that's what I'm feeling right now. Jim and the kids would convince me to give it a try.

Maybe I won't even get to retire. Maybe this will be a fast growing cancer. A cruel fate.

Then I remember, for a moment, how the body is supposed to be symmetrical on both sides, harmonious. If something is on one side, then it's often on the other side: knee caps, eyes, fingers, and wrist bones. The list goes on and on. So, I feel the other side of my head behind my right ear. I shift my hands on the steering wheel and, lo and behold, I have the same lump behind my right ear! This is a miracle since it appears not to be a twin cancer but part of my skeletal system. Maybe it is just a bone. Maybe, in fact, I don't have cancer. Maybe I won't die before I retire. I feel again, switching my hands, as I glide, no longer morosely or tearfully, down the hill. Yes, this is bone. This is bone. I'm made of bone, and this happens to be one of those bones. The thighbone is connected to the hip bone; the knee bone is connected to the shinbone. I'm singing now like I used to do in elementary school. "The thighbone connected to the shinbone. The ear bone connected to the head bone." I'm making up my own words. I'm so happy! Yes, hear the word of the Lord. Thank you, Lord. Maybe I will get to retire.

That last week as I pack up my office, fear and joy live side by side.

A New Life and Celebrating

I talk to my sister on the phone when I get home. "Focus on what you want," she says when I spout my usual anxiety about life and leaving my job. Okay. I'm focusing on my new healthy body. Soon, I will make sure to get some sun every day. Vitamin D is being slurped into my skin like dust in a vacuum cleaner. I'm taking my vitamin C. I'm eating a lot of fruits and vegetables, all colors of the rainbow. I'm glowing in the dark, not from radiation but from antioxidants. I'm healthy. I'll make it to retirement. I'm so close I can almost touch it.

Jim is running an errand. Penny is lying on the laundry I need to fold and put away this weekend. She's all decked out in her forest green coat that was made by our friend Louise. Penny has four coats now. Jim likes the forest green, though I often choose the purple one. She looks so unbelievably relaxed. I watch as her chest rises and falls in perfect balance. I suddenly understand why dogs lower your blood pressure.

Outside in the garden, I look at stairs Jim built that lead to a stone wall he uncovered. So much beauty hidden under other things. Life is discovery—like finding the Nina's in the *New York Times* datebook section when I was a child, an artist who loved his daughter so much that he put her name on his drawings, hidden and for us to find, or the tiny monkeys and people hidden in trees in children's magazines at the dentist's office. So much inside other things. I wonder what Penny dreams about? What is it to be healthy? To live cradled in the moment? To live surprised in the moment? To feel your breath move in and out, so easily? To leave a job that overwhelms your body and finally pay attention? To listen. To heal.

The next week, I set aside time to visit my friend Amber, who was in two of my creative writing classes and then became an editor at a small publishing house. She's just had a baby, and I want to see him and hold him. I want to see her, too, of course, but babies always take center stage. This feels like time I'm stealing away from grading all the end-of-the-year papers.

When I visit Amber and precious little Henrik, Amber says there were definite reasons he cried: when he had a wet diaper, when he had gas, when he was hungry. That was it. Otherwise, he's a happy baby, she says, and I certainly can feel that. I marvel at the way he seems so at peace in the crook of my arm, the tiny valentine smile, the fleshy baby arms just beginning to reach out into the world to hold a golden bow on the gift I brought.

And then like clockwork, after we had tea and chatted, his lips move toward an invisible breast. At sixty-one, it's been a long time since I've had milk flowing like honey into my children's waiting mouths and tummies, so he gets passed back to mom. But that breastfeeding time is like no other time. A memory flashes across my mind. A wonderful woman, Ruth—whose daughter-in-law Pat became one of my best friends—was in my poetry class at the Home for Jewish Parents and said she wanted to go out for dinner. A friend and I broke her out of the home one evening (all legal) and took her to a restaurant. Little did we know, it was to be the night before she died. "One of the best memories of my life is breastfeeding my children. I can feel their small bodies. I can feel them sucking on my nipple," she said. Ruth was ninety years old then, her skin sagging, wrinkles creasing her face, but that night I saw the young woman proudly holding her son to her breast. The next day she died.

John R. talked about meditating; John L., about spending precious time with his daughter; Eleanor about finally writing; Betsy about taking walks with friends; Jim about creating art. In the last month, the door has swung open to a new life. Life begins to change, a visceral change you can feel inside your body.

I leave Amber and Henrik to go home and do some work, which seems to elude me today. I can't even begin one of the many stacks. Stacks. I wish they were stacks of pancakes dripping with maple syrup.

When I return home from Amber's, Jim is about to leave the house. "I'm going out to the Sutro Baths," he says, "when the tide is low," because supposedly you can see some shipwrecks there. He's got a backpack filled with water and the video camera. He's been retired two years, and only in the second year, the artist that he is started to emerge again. He's taking a lot of photos and videos. He continues to work on his ceramic table. The table will be proudly displayed in our garden where he will lie in the hammock—when it's warm enough in San Francisco, which means about five days out of the year—put down his beer as he watches humming birds speed by, and then sleep to the sounds of chirping. Now, he is leaving out the door. I can't go because of THE PAPERS—the papers that have consumed my life—"Be careful, Mon Cher," I call out as he descends the steps. "Be careful of the high tide," I call out to him. He is not a water guy and has had dreams of drowning off a ship.

"That's why I'm going now at 1:30," he says, "at low tide." Penny barks madly as he leaves.

I'm resting today. A stomachache of the past week has finally started to subside, the tenseness softening, but I'm tired. I'm putting off finishing an evaluation of a colleague, grading King Lear presentations, and recording the last paper grades in the computer—all tedious tasks. But, I still love my students and want to do well by them.

Suddenly, Penny whines and goes to the French door where Jim has created a beautiful garden, rock walls he unearthed from years of hiding that look like England or Ireland. The steps go up to three separate decks where you can look over the house. He loves to be on top of things like Twin Peaks or the tops of other mountains and look down while I am more of a water person. Penny is still crying. I'm trying to rest but get up as I think she might have to pee. I open the door. Sunlight washes over us. "Do it," I say to her—the code name for "pee." She wanders to the side of the deck where she usually pees, turns around, stands for a while, then walks by the stone wall, and decides to go inside. She doesn't pee.

"I think you just wanted to go out and smell the flowers," I say to her as she scurries into the house. She seems to nod in agreement. She walks down the hallway and finds the one slanted ray of sun on the wooden floor and plops her furry body down. I lie down on the bed.

I'll put on my relaxation tape for thirty minutes before I finally do my work.

Today, I saw a new baby; today, I remembered the pleasure of breastfeeding my own tiny, perfect daughters; today, I stood in the sunlight for five minutes on Waller Street before climbing the stairs to see my friend and her baby. Today, Jim went to see the wreckage of a ship floating in the ocean. Today, my dog wanted to go outside among the rocks, the wooden deck, just to be outside, her black nostrils flared, her eyes saturated with the green plant world. Soon I will be retired from my full-time job. I'll hand in my parking sticker. I'll hand in my keys. I'll close the door to my office, finally and forever.

It's the last Monday of the last week of school. I park my car. The campus seems empty and gray. The weather has been on the verge of showers all day. I buy tea at the truck. "You're almost there now!" a colleague says to me. "Are you counting the days?" I smile, and we chat. Then I run into the ex-secretary of the English Department, now working in the Art Department. "Blaise is going to high school next year. He's 5'4" already." I remember him as a cute, hyperactive six-year-old.

"You're doing the right thing," she says. "It will all work out." She's reading my anxious mind.

I go back to my office and then up to the English Department on the fifth floor to pay for a rabbit cheese plate and knives I bought at a benefit auction. The secretary's granddaughter is there, and I talk with her about the rabbit's long ears. She's making a coffee cup into a drum. I wish I could play with her all morning instead of going to class.

In class, students present their research topics. Chairs are in a semicircle. We can all see each other, now, at the end of the semester and the end of all my semesters here. They've worked hard on their environmental papers, and I'm proud of them. They're motivated—talking about the Amazon rainforest, gorilla poaching, protecting sharks, and the nuclear disaster in Japan. My student with traumatic brain injury, which he received while on duty in Iraq, is sitting in the circle. I remember when he came into my office.

"By the way, I have traumatic brain injury," he said as he walked out the door.

"I'll get you through the class," I said, looking directly at him.

"We'll see," he said, his head down.

And now he's here, in the circle.

After the class is over, I pick up my books and purse and leave the room. The hallways are empty because it's the final exam period. I pass by bulletin boards, mostly empty now until the summer session starts. I walk down two flights of stairs to my office, Batmale 369, and open the door. For a minute, I hold my keys in my hand and look at the door key—look at the grooves, the particular grooves of this unique key I've used for many, many years. Next week, I will turn in my key to the secretary. Give her a hug. Walk down the long hallway. Hear the door to the English Department shut behind me. I hear all the voices of students and colleagues I've loved start to vanish. How do I fill the void?

Visions of my black journals—the old poetry and prose from the past and new blank pages that I will fill—give me energy. I walk up the stairs to my car, my step lighter as I envision my new life. I drive down the serpentine road for the last time and breathe deeply. I've done it. I'm alive, very, very alive.

For many, those last moments can be exhilarating. But for those who were downsized or for those, like my nephew George, who left because of disability, the last moments can be filled with anger at being discarded or resentment at the body breaking down. However, even in these difficult situations, people can find a lot to live for in this new phase. George's boss told him to "start reading and learning." He spends a lot of time at bookstores and libraries and has become an avid reader. He watches the History Channel, visits museums, and recently took a trip with his wife to Pennsylvania to see a famous Frank Lloyd Wright house.

People can be forced out of their jobs due to any number of reasons. They depend on working for a certain numbers of years to boost their Social Security payments or a 401K account. It can be extremely difficult to have your retirement dreams derailed. But, sometimes, new opportunities appear as people leave an oppressive job. As with everything in life—and as my life-coaching, now psychotherapist, sister reminds me—focus on what you want; not everyone has the perfect retirement.

Celebrations

For some, there seems to be endless parties with family and friends. Others go more quietly into this new life. The English Department always has an end-of-the-year dinner to honor retirees and new hires. The cycle of life. I felt wistful sitting at a table with colleagues I'd known for many, many years. The retirees, including me, all gave speeches. As I looked out at the sea of faculty and staff and spoke about my years there, I remember feeling loved by my colleagues and grateful for all my years at City College of San Francisco. I added that all who graded papers should take good care of their necks. Eleanor was feted by her colleagues at Kaiser, and Betsy E. had a huge celebration with San Francisco supervisors attending. For others, like Jim, the parties can feel overwhelming, though he knew he would return as a volunteer. These celebrations also can feel surreal.

One way of dealing with "the end" is to plan something you love to do for the week after retirement. It can be simple, such as going to a bookstore and browsing, sitting at a local cafe you rarely visit and reading a great book, or going to a midafternoon Giant's baseball game as Jim did on the day after he retired. Some people plan a trip—a cruise, a visit to friends or family, or a camping expedition. These special celebrations or moments are like a bookmark, separating one part of your life from the next.

You have confronted your deepest fears and retired from your job. Whatever time you have left on this earth, you can begin to fill it by doing some of the things that make you happy. Pick up a leaf that has fallen from the ground. Read a book you've wanted to read for years. Visit a new state or country. Sit with friends at a local cafe. Go on a hike, feel calmed by the tall branches of trees. Pet your precious pets, their purrs and relaxed bodies, relaxing you. Hug children, grandchildren, and friends. Paint a picture, take a photo, write a book. Travel to a national park. Take a long walk on city streets or a long walk by the beach. Even if you have to do part-time work or regularly take care of grandchildren or elderly parents, make sure to fit in these new activities, things you have longed to do, into your new life.

Breathe in to the count of four and out to the count of eight.

My nervous system, which used to hum loudly like those huge electrical wires, is now much calmer. I'm proud of all I gave to so many students over so many years; however, I'm happy that Jim and I now have a little time to travel and relax. We're very lucky. Sometimes I wonder if we would still be healthy had we stayed at our jobs for much longer. I know I got out at the right time and hope other older people can make the decision to leave a job that has become oppressive and still have some healthy, calmer years in their sixth, seventh, eighth, or even ninth decade of life.

THE FIRST THREE YEARS AFTER RETIREMENT

How do I adjust to my new life? How do I reclaim what I love to do? How do I set up a structure for my days?

YEAR ONE

How can I have feelings of exhilaration and new found freedom along with feelings of displacement? How do I want to fill my days? What's the best way to create a schedule?

On May 28, 2011, I officially retire. On my Facebook page when I post my retirement news, one friend responds, "Welcome to the world of possibilities." Another writes, "Now your neck won't feel like it is going to shatter from grading papers." In the first week, Jim and I go across the Golden Gate Bridge on a *weekday*—such a free feeling— on a hike to Pt. Reyes National Seashore by the Pacific Ocean. We drive to Marin County through the Rainbow Tunnel (now called the Robin Williams tunnel) and we both hear echoes of our young children and their high-pitched voices, saying "Rainbow Tunnel, Rainbow Tunnel" when we went camping or traveled to Tennessee Valley Road, a mile hike to the ocean, past a horse stable, sometimes hawks circling the sky.

My mind is calmer, no longer making financial calculations for retirement. I don't need to call State Teacher's Retirement System again and again, wondering about the .5 percent that might or might not be recalculated and could add or subtract thousands and thousands of dollars over all the years I will live on my retirement payout. I signed a million times on the dotted lines. And I'm healthy. That's huge. I can walk for miles. I'm fortunate to have Jim by my side. So many couples don't make it this far for various reasons: divorce, growing apart, illness, or death. Jim and I have been fortunate to make it through raising children, various struggles, the stress of work, and then the stress of retirement. My fears that I will die or that Jim will die before retirement seem to have receded. We still love each other and actually have things to talk about. We take a selfie on the beach. I notice the extra lines in my face. My hair is too long and raggedy, the T-shirt I'm wearing has been hiding in my drawer for over ten years, slightly frayed, but who cares. We're in the great outdoors. Jim takes off his glasses for the photo, and we both lean toward each other. I drink in the moment. We walk down the beach, marveling at the cliff faces and looking out to sea, both silent for a minute. Tiny birds scuttle across the sand like ice skaters. A hawk circles the sky, so majestic, like royalty of the air.

What I find truly liberating is all the things I *don't* have to think about: financial calculations for one. It's done. No more lists on paper. My pension is my pension. Jim's Social Security is his Social Security. Period. Although I will look for teaching, I've decided not to teach credit courses part-time at City College. My neck screams at the thought of grading papers again. The decision is made. No more flip-flops. No more should I or shouldn't I. At Pt. Reyes, the ocean air mists my skin. I breathe in the scent of sea salt, a memory from my East Coast childhood spent at Jones Beach and Riis Park. I take a really deep breath, a post-retirement breath. Jim and I lie back against the cliff and eat our lunch as we look out to sea. The drive back is easy, not as much traffic during the day, and we come home greeted by Penny who does a little circle dance of celebration that we're home, even at her advanced age.

It's good to plan short excursions with special people in your life after retirement. These short trips, like the one Jim and I did to Pt. Reyes, can now become part of the "every week" if not the "every day." My sister has a solid group of women friends who meet every weekend at the beach. She lives in St. Thomas, so meeting at the beach is quite convenient. For those with children and grandchildren nearby, it's good to set up a schedule—a weekly lunch with a child or a weekly visit to take care of grandchildren. Anna set up a weekly time to see her grandchildren when she retired. "It's important as they grow up so fast." Years ago, we used to do Expression Night and have people over once a month to read a poem, play a piece on the piano, or do fruit art, as one friend did. We're thinking of doing that again, a gathering of people.

It's also good to have something special to do or just time to relax, to ease into the transition. Betsy E. went on a family vacation in Hawaii a month after retirement. She could unwind, surrounded by loved ones. John L. said he focused on fitness and health. He started running three times a week and set up a gym in his house. He could finally work on having a balanced life. Anna joined a sports club. John R. said he started riding a mountain bike. Eleanor said she slept for three months. The pure, unadulterated exhaustion that sets in at the end of retirement, both physical and emotional, can linger. How wonderful it is to lounge in bed and not to set the alarm clock; sit at the breakfast table in your pajamas as you linger over the paper; read (anything and everything); take a walk and come back for a short nap in the afternoon. Pampering yourself for a while can also help.

If your job was chronically stressful, there can be what's called the "let-down effect." In the middle of meeting a huge deadline or giving final grades and or finishing up a creative project, people can feel fine as they push themselves to get to the finish line. However, how many times have we gotten sick on a vacation when we relax? Or ended up at home with a cold on the weekend after going full-throttle all week? Medical experts talk about the rise in cortisol, the stress hormone during a busy period. When the cortisol drops, however, it can set off an inflammatory response. When people actually retire, their bodies and minds have often been revved up for a while as they sign documents, say goodbye to colleagues, clean their offices, and sometimes stare into the void with all the "what do I do now" thoughts that threaten to short-circuit their brains. That's why it's good to do something relaxing after retirement, just as couples often take honeymoons after the stress of a wedding.

John L. said he felt guilty that he wasn't doing much after he retired, but he needed the downtime. He had been going so fast for so long on the merry-go-round of work. He took up sailing and threw himself into this new hobby as he relished not boarding planes all the time and not missing out on his daughter's life. He could be there for her. Eleanor, finally rested, emerged from her cocoon and went on a trip to New Orleans to dance and began a romance with her new love, Mo. "It was a very romantic time."

On the day after he retired, Jim went to see his beloved Giant's baseball team play during the day, an unbelievable treat to himself, a reward as he moved into a new phase of life. His favorite pitcher, Tim Lincecum, was pitching. He had tickets right behind home plate and overheard one woman saying, "Why doesn't Timmy get his hair cut and his teeth straightened?" Jim snickered to himself. Lincecum is one of the best-loved pitchers in baseball.

However, the rest of the day didn't go as planned. On the way home, before getting on the BART, he passed a sidewalk cafe where an elderly, intoxicated man, over 200 pounds, stood up, moved precariously from side to side and lost his balance and fell toward Jim. Jim, who at 5'7" and 155 pounds could not compare to this man's weight and girth, instinctively ran toward the man and reached out to break his fall. He imagined the man crashing on to the pavement and fracturing his skull. Instead of falling on to the pavement, the man fell directly, with all of his massive weight, on to Jim's left hand and thumb. He let the man lie down and asked, "Are you alright?" Then he added, "Because I'm not." Someone called an ambulance, and the man was whisked away, saved by Jim.

Unfortunately, Jim's thumb was fractured and never healed correctly. It has bothered him ever since. To this day, years later, Jim looks back and sees it as a dream omen. He thinks of this man as a ghostlike figure. *You have to take care of yourself. You don't need to be helping older people all the time.* "Perhaps it's time for people to help me," he says. "I can finally take a break from my role as caregiver." It's important to know your limits, especially as you get older. As Dirty Harry said, "A man has to know his limitations." That becomes more real as we age. Jim began taking care of himself more. That incident was a lesson in what he needed to do to ensure he stayed healthy in retirement.

Months before I retired, I had planned a trip to go back east to visit some dear friends and family and go on a book tour. The combination was exhilarating. I would get to connect with those I love deeply and also get out into the world as an author. Our daughter Sarah moved into our house to take care of our pooch, a great relief as Penny was getting older and harder to leave, her liquid brown eyes devastatingly sad as we descended the stairs. We heard her whining all the way out the door. She adored Sarah, though, so we knew she would quickly get over our leaving.

My memoir about the explosion that burned my parents had recently been published, so I had readings set up in a number of places—a couple in Cape Cod—where the accident happened in the summer of 1954. Through a friend of my sister's, a journalist and photographer was to go with me and Jim as I searched for the house that exploded that fateful summer. I had not seen it since I was carried across the dirt road at four years old.

We walk on to the beach and look back at the houses. "Is this the place?" the journalist asks, "The beach you walked to every day." I feel like it is, that I'm "hot" like the "cold and hot" game we played as children, but I don't see "our house." She snaps some photos of my slightly gray hair blowing in the wind and then we trudge up rickety steps, just like the ones I remembered when I was four. As we walk by a few small houses, my stomach begins to churn. Then I see it, a strange wooden pole in front of a small house that looks like the right one. "But it's not brick!" I announce to my husband.

"Look more closely," he says. I see the brick is painted white. That pole, still there fifty-eight years later, was where my father's bathrobe still hung the morning after the explosion. It was burned and looked like the carbon paper in my mother's desk drawer. The firefighters had not removed it. The morning after my parents were burned, my sister and I looked at the robe, the shell of my father, and held each other's hands.

The photographer snaps the photo of my horror-stricken face.

This is my moment of fame. Jim and I walk into a nearby coffee shop, islanders in their khakis and docksider shoes and see the *Cape Cod Times* spread out over all the tables, my horror-stricken face on the front page. I want to shout, "That's me!" My need for adulation and praise is being met far from home. "Mom and Dad," even though they died many years before, "Look! I'm on the cover of the newspaper. I'm telling your story!" I can see them nodding from on high. They were not much into outward signs of praise and adulation. A nod was quite something.

I had set up other readings as well and was interviewed on National Public Radio in Woods Hole, Massachusetts, by Mindy Todd—one of the best interviewers I've ever met. I had worked on my memoir for over fifteen years, a long and difficult gestation both emotionally and physically. I dealt with panic attacks triggered by the trauma of that time. I was teaching full-time, raising children, and searching for agents, editors, and publishers. I had a passion. Retirement for me meant I could leap into the world I loved and that my stories could also leap through thin membranes of fear and get out into the world, too.

That summer, Jim and I also visit New York City, amble around Greenwich Village where I grew up, spending two full afternoons at the Metropolitan Museum of Art seeing an Egyptian temple, incredible reliefs as well as Impressionist art. We go to a favorite pizzeria and Italian restaurant, meet old friends, and spend time with my mother's best friend, Penny, still working and going strong at ninety-one years old. I feel a moment of guilt that I retired so early. How come she's still working? I'm only sixty-one (almost sixty-two). Am I lazy, a slacker? Then I remember I need to trust myself. This is the right decision for *me*—for my writing, for my neck, for my mental health. Penny didn't take her Social Security until she was eighty-six. But, she is like the bionic woman or an Olympic athlete. They're just made differently. She also grew up with a mother who was a Christian Scientist. She can talk her body into health. "It's all in my genes," she chuckles, but I'm not so sure.

After New York City, we climb aboard the Amtrak train to Connecticut, the landscape changing from concrete sidewalks and high rises to leafy trees. We stay with my stepdaughter, Bonnie, son-in-law, George, and our precious grandchildren, Quinn, Tait, and Reed. I do a reading at the local independent bookstore that Bonnie arranges. We take our three grandkids to a science museum and an art museum and out for sundaes, watching them happily slurp up chocolate fudge, butterscotch, and whipped cream, a sugar overload from their grandparents. We go to the kids' sporting events and swim at the local club. And as if that isn't enough, I decide to check my website mail that week in Connecticut, which I don't do that much, and see "You Won a Prize." *Right*, I think cynically to myself. It's some time-share ad or a drawing for a car or a scam. I'm so glad I opened it. The Wisconsin Library Association chose my memoir for its award. If I hadn't clicked open, then, the prize would have gone to someone else. Vanished. Things are really looking up. By leaps and bounds, I'm entering my new life.

After goodbyes to our family in Connecticut, we board the Amtrak again, this time headed for Buffalo, Jim's hometown. I always feel gloomy as I get farther away from New York City. Perhaps as we get older, the homing-pigeon syndrome gets even stronger; even the concrete heat and the sickly smell of cotton candy at the 14th Street subway stop have folded themselves forever into my soul. I'm retired. Now it's time to move home. But, Jim has his feet solidly planted in San Francisco. New York City has not entered his soul. Although he's better each time we visit the Big A, I made the mistake of taking us back down to the village on the subway at rush hour. The crunch of people did not amuse him. As he gripped the pole to steady himself with hundreds of others stuffed into the subway car, I could see actual pain on his face. When the doors opened at 8th Street, he finally relaxed.

For some retirees, the homing-pigeon instinct gets so strong, and people actually do move back to places where they grew up. They remember the smells of the corner bakery, eating napoleons or chocolate éclairs, or the autumn chill in the air, or the sounds of voices, now long gone. For some, if close friends and relatives still live there, a move could work, but as the writer Thomas Wolfe said, "You can never go home again." Places change. People change, too, in ways that aren't easily quantifiable. It's important to really research and check out those places before you impulsively pack up a lifetime of memories, rent a U-Haul, and return home to find it is not really home. For some, especially when they leave places where they have a rent-controlled apartment or own a home, it can be near financially impossible to ever return.

I begin working on a new book on the train, another memoir. I can have the retirement I want. Jim's huge and loving family welcomes us, and I give a reading at Talking Leaves, the independent bookstore on Main Street. I'm honored. Grateful. I feel free, unencumbered by thinking about the next semester—classes to prepare, stacks of papers that would wait for me every week and weekend. I'm out in the world as a writer. I don't even feel sad at all when I think of not seeing my colleagues. I'll make some lunch dates.

A little while after we return from the East Coast, fall begins. September, with the beginning of the school year, floods my mind with memories of buying pencils and fleshy pink erasers when I was small. Lately, every fall I've bought notebooks for each class—and before online grading—grade books, meticulously entering the names of often over 100 students a semester. I'm aware of flex day at the college, when everyone takes workshops from meditation to how to help English as a Second Language (ESL) students move into regular English classes. I feel pangs of missing my colleagues; I can visualize myself by the food truck schmoozing with friends, deciding which doughnut to pick, and filling my cup with coffee before I go into the Diego Rivera Theater to hear the chancellor speak. But, I'm getting ready for something new as well. In another week, I begin my two days a week stint at the San Francisco Writer's Grotto where I will work on two new projects, surrounded by journalists, novelists, memoirists, and poets.

I calm myself during this time by taking more walks with my dog in Glen Park Canyon, right across the street from our home. We pass the street named Paradise and enter the mouth of the park. Penny, though she's an old girl, is a real trooper and troops with me farther and farther with joy in her inky eyes and her fifteen-pound body keeping pace. Sometimes, we sit on a bench and watch the humans and the dogs mix, a clot of women with coffee cups and dogs, all gathering together, a lone man jogging with a T-shirt that reads, "Latitude Adjustment." On occasion, I put on headphones in the early morning and go out by myself on the path through the eucalyptus trees, speed walking to Linda Rondstadt or Bob Dylan around a winding path three times, past the place where my children used to go to a city camp and explore among the rocks. The children wear colored scarves according to their ages and climb the boulders that line the canyon. I have nowhere I need to be at a specific time. Being outdoors more makes me feel lighter, surrounded by the smell of eucalyptus, the bark peeling like banana leaves, surrounded by men, women, children, and dogs enjoying the park. I even buy myself some new sneakers with good treads. I'm getting healthy, as well, doing what I love. Nature is a wonderful healer, and many retirees set up regular walks with friends and neighbors.

My first day at the Grotto, I put my computer, a piece of fruit, a box of lentil soup, my cords for the computer and phone all in a used backpack and take the BART downtown and then walk the many blocks down 2nd Street to the Grotto. I pass a sign, "Working alone sucks: Shared office space in this building." This sign speaks to the human need for community. Writers often work alone for hours and hours. Kafka said, "Writing is utter solitude, the descent into the cold abyss of oneself." I don't want to feel like I'm in a cold abyss. I want to be part of a community. I need colleagues, people to schmooze with. The first time I do the walk, it's daunting. I keep thinking, like a little kid, "Are we there yet?" The straps of the backpack cut into my shoulders. The traffic is crazy, drivers not looking carefully as they make right turns on red lights. Years later, when I find out my smart phone tracks the distance I walk, I realize it's almost a mile from the BART to the Grotto door. How can I keep carrying this load all that distance? As time goes on, I get a lighter computer and a rolling suitcase.

When I enter the Grotto, I see book covers framed on a wall from *New York Times* best-selling memoirs to a book on mental health in America to travel anthologies, books of poetry, books of short stories, books on how the food industry is killing us, and books on the power of verbs—all written by Grotto authors in their offices and carrels on the second floor of a downtown San Francisco office building. To the left of the front door are all the mailboxes and a black leather couch where packages are stacked up on top of each other. This is a living, breathing place and I wonder how I will find my place in it.

I follow the woman, who is orienting me, to the kitchen. "Two microwaves," she says, "and this is the refrigerator." A hot water dispenser seems to be the focal point of the counter with a pink dispense and unlock button. It's quite large, so caffeine-seeking creators can fill and refill for a while. Now I know where I can get coffee and store my lunch. I'm shown the "Chore List" prominently displayed on one of the cabinets and soon will be assigned a chore: from kitchen/compost/garbage duty to reading manuscripts sent in by potential "Grotto Fellows" who come for three months. We leave the kitchen, and she shows me the conference room. "We gather for lunch at around noon," she says, and I breathe a sigh of relief. I'll meet people and maybe make some new friends. Photos of "Grottoites" fill a huge bulletin board, and I look at their faces. I recognize no one except one person who has helped shepherd me into the Grotto. My photo will be placed on the bulletin board in the conference room.

The carrel I choose today is by the front door—perhaps it's where I want to be—not quite in or out, a free-floating feeling. A black bookcase filled with classics like *1984* and *Jane Eyre* along with books about herbs and illness and writing are stacked next to each other. A bulletin board by these front carrels has biographies of all the freelancers. "Yours will go up there too," my orienter says. I feel a moment of pride and stand up taller. I'm a freelancer at the Grotto. My bio will be up there. But mainly I'm feeling lost, missing home and Jim and Penny. When I go to the conference room for lunch, I search the faces of all these strangers for the faces of all my friends in City College. Will I make new friends? I hope so. For many retirees, when they begin something new, like a volunteer position, the new faces and the strange environment can often feel unsettling.

I diligently go back to my carrel and begin, again, to write and, more importantly, remember why I'm here.

In the book *Being Mortal*, author Atul Gawande focuses on illness and the end of life and how we die. However, the book is also about how we live, particularly during the last phase of our lives. He says, "The chance to shape one's story is essential to sustaining meaning in life . . ." For me, this act of writing, of doing what I love, is my chance now to shape my life. Everyone, if they get to retire or even retire part-time, has a chance at shaping their life. How do I want to fill my days? What will give me happiness and enrich my life? For everyone, of course, it's different. It's important to do something everyday that gives you great pleasure.

On one of the first days at the Grotto, the sun is shining, and I decide to take a walk and explore the neighborhood. The Grotto is near AT&T Park—the Giant's baseball field—and also only a block away from South Park, which has a few restaurants. I walk out of the dark building into the sun a block down and to the right to a small park surrounded by a few trendy cafes and restaurants. At the park, children race after a ball, but this is mostly an adult hangout filled with twenty- to thirty-year-olds plugged into smartphones, some talking to each other between gazing at texts and using a thumb flexion to respond that must have come from some alien universe. I have never mastered that. Some rush past me, as I sit on a bench, carrying take-out cartons from a nearby restaurant.

Like my precious dog, I search for slants of light. It's chilly in the park, so I find a concrete ledge of a building and sit quietly, letting my skin swallow rays of light. A few small dogs walk by attached to owners not moving quite as fast. The dogs sniff and look for food dropped on the ground. Trees frame the street. This street reminds me of Greenwich Village where I grew up. But where are the people I know? The hellos and goodbyes? I overhear conversations about "deals" and 1:00 p.m. meetings. For a minute, I feel panicky, detached from these people, this digital world, this non-retired world—single people walking fast with a purpose, or two or three people talking together, most of them twenty to thirty years my junior. Who am I now? Sitting by a stop sign on a ledge of concrete, are my old selves now meaningless?

I'm here to write, I remind myself, again like a mantra. I'm here to write in this new geography with new faces. As I lumber my detached self back to the Grotto, a young man passes with a Kent State University sweatshirt. He's about twenty-three years old. When I hear Kent State, I think only of the student massacre in 1970, that tragic and pivotal moment in history. Does anyone around here even know about that? Probably, but I feel very alone in my sixty-one-year-old body. I pass a taqueria and glance at the offerings. I'm trying never to eat lunch out for my new budget; I pass an industrial looking office building. A lone black pigeon scuttles across the sidewalk to the door. I laugh for a minute, imagining a Disney movie and the pigeon is looking for a job as he climbs steps to a glass door and then suddenly flies away.

I walk back to 2nd Street, my constitutional over. I take the elevator up to the Grotto and write again, words flowing out of me. I have a schedule, two days a week at the Grotto. A plan. My Grotto days are written on my calendar that hangs on one side of the fridge.

Many people who first retire need and want some kind of schedule. A schedule can be grounding. Betsy E. throws herself into community projects as she has always done, but now she has time to do them. Anna joins a gardening club. Dixie has regular times she watches her twin grandsons. Jim keeps up his running schedule, necessary for his physical and mental health. He also volunteers at the senior center where he worked. Others volunteer or even go back to their place of work, one day a week as John R. did. He can see patients in a much less stressful way. It's important to remember that it can take time to ease into this new phase of life.

YEAR TWO

Is your schedule working for you? How do you handle feelings of overwhelm and calm yourself? How do you sort out what you need to do and what you want to do, making time for yourself?

When we return from the trip, a new reality sets in. I left early from my job. My pension, though I'm eternally grateful that I actually have a pension, will not pay all our bills, especially the mortgage and equity line. Before I left, I had applied to teach in MFA low-residency programs and spent a lot of time getting my recommendations together. None of those jobs came through. I thought we could just make it—in fact, that was a stretch. In addition, we're helping our older daughter with rent as she attends an MFA program in grad school.

We're more than fortunate to own a house. "We can rent out our house for a year and move to Buffalo," I say to Jim one day after doing the bills. Something needs to shift. I know that. Jim definitely doesn't want to leave San Francisco permanently; the thought makes him shudder; however, we think about a temporary move and even interview a family who might take our house for a year. "We can get ahead; pay down bills; start a savings account." I check out what rentals would cost in Buffalo. I went to grad school there and have some close writer friends there and, of course, we would have Jim's huge extended family. I could take the train to New York City. It could happen though it's freezing in Buffalo. The thought of scraping frozen snow off a buried car sends chills up Jim's spine. But, as it turns out, no one is interested in the rental. Of course we can sell the house. We're fortunate to have options. I imagine myself taking classes, going to the gym, writing, and not waking up and looking at our bank account every day.

Whenever I mention selling the house to Jim, downsizing either in the area or moving to a place where the cost of living is cheaper, Jim grows visibly upset. "I've worked on every inch of this house," he says, "and the garden." He does not want to leave San Francisco. And in the end, neither do I. Both our children are in California. We don't know where we would go.

I know we need more of the green stuff than what would be coming in from my pension and Jim's Social Security. We can rent out a room. That could be the ticket. Jim starts working endlessly on the house, day by day fixing things. He fixes drawers that have broken, changes light bulbs, renovates a bathroom, and even fixes dry rot, learning how to do some of the more complicated tasks by watching YouTube videos over and over. For days, he makes patterns on butcher paper that will guide him as he puts the tiles on our bathroom floor. He's dyslexic so this helps him. He's numbered the squares like paint-by-number paintings for children. Later, I see him slumped over the computer watching another YouTube video and hitting the replay button. He also works tirelessly on the garden, carting loads of weeds through the house as that is the only access to the front. "My job is to maintain the house like a ship," he says, "No dry rot, no threatening leaks." He even regrouted the bathroom tiles. "I don't do plumbing," he says. We call in our wonderful plumber, Larry, who talks non-stop. Jim gets the house in shipshape. The bathroom he renovates is a work of art, pale green walls, black-and-white tiles, and Uncle Bill's paintings gracing the walls.

Jim's dreams of becoming an artist and spending hours in his art room—one of the kid's old bedrooms—begin to fade. He made a ceramic table there and some reliefs with hieroglyphics. He is a trooper, though, and works tirelessly on our home. He continues to run three times a week and visits museums regularly. "Museums are like my private clubs," he says. It's not exactly the retirement he imagined, but he does things every day that he loves.

We also begin divesting things, putting out our allowed ten items for curbside pickup and take clothes and books to the Salvation Army. Many retirees do huge cleanings. Cleaning can create psychological space in our minds and hearts. As retirees enter this new phase of life, it's great to keep only what truly matters—and that's different for everyone. Our garage is filled with a huge cotton candy machine we bought our younger daughter in high school, and my mother's sewing books that I never used (as sewing must have skipped a generation). Plus, most manuals are online now. We don't need the sewing books. We need to ask Laura about her old cotton candy machine. Maybe donate it? Why don't I just get rid of the sewing books? Is it because I want to think of my mother and all her expert sewing projects? Even with terribly burned hands, she managed to sew coats and dresses—even a smocked dress for my daughter Sarah. However, keeping her sewing books doesn't make any sense. My mother was also great at decluttering, and her voice from up-high definitely wants me to give them to someone who will actually sew more than a button on a coat.

I have an aversion to getting rid of my books, but how many of my hundreds of poetry collections will I actually read in my lifetime? Having a few open shelves in the garage will help me breathe more deeply. My asthma kicks up down there. But, I have little time to clean our garage, which remains a disaster area. We need to clean the upstairs.

From a semi-slob, to a medium slob, to a semi-neatnik—my progression over the years—I am not prepared to be a total neatnik, which is required if you are renting out a room in your house and especially when you rent out the whole house, which we would do a year from then, registering with the city and getting a business license. Renting out a room, particularly when you serve breakfast, means the kitchen area and the living room also have to be in perfect shape. No more piles of laundry on the living room couch or books and papers on the dining room table, at least when guests rent a room. I become obnoxiously neat, even to myself. I notice places no one would ever see, where paint has been chipped, or a tiny dust ball hides like a criminal under a cabinet in the TV area where most guests would not enter.

The bathroom is perhaps the most difficult to keep clean. If one tiny hair is lying on the floor, that might ruin our stellar reviews. A hair in the bathroom? But how do you really get out every single piece of hair in the bathroom? I wet a paper towel and search frantically like a detective for an unwanted hair and attack it, smiling to see the hair on the paper towel and gone from the floor. But have I gotten every hair? Spider webs are another no-no. We had one guest who said a spider dropped into the bathtub. Fortunately, he still gave us a great review. I walk around with a broom—searching like a lighthouse light for spider webs—and apologize to the spiders before I strike. The webs are so intricate, so spectacular, but they must be gone, deleted from the house.

Not everyone will rent out rooms in their homes or take in roommates, but it is becoming more common for seniors to earn extra income that way. For many, their home is their only asset. The National Council on Aging says, "Over twenty-five million Americans aged sixty and over are economically insecure." Renting out a room, if that is possible, can be a lifeline. There are also programs to help seniors get jobs, often as caretakers for children or others who are ill. For many, after paying the bills, there is nothing left over or, worse, people go into debt.

Along with renting out a room every once in a while, I search for teaching jobs. I have "hire me" written across my face. I tell all my friends I'm looking for part-time teaching. One day while taking the BART to the Grotto, I run into Susan, a mother from the high school my kids attended. I have a vague memory that she runs a program that hires teachers. And she does. She needs a memoir teacher, six-week stints at UC Berkeley. I get hired. Then I have coffee with a friend, and she needs a creative writing teacher for a night class at Notre Dame University. ASAP. Then my friend Leslie tells me that the City College non-credit program needs a replacement for the women's literature teacher. Bingo. I have three teaching jobs and I've already set up private workshops in my house. I bow my head to the higher powers of teaching and money that have rained all this good fortune on me. It can be tough out there for older people with age discrimination. Often the best way to get part-time work is through your network, letting everyone you know that you are looking for part-time work.

Over the next two years, I am no longer a full-time employee and tethered to City College. I never have endless papers to grade; I only have to give grades in one small class, and my neck feels better and better, yet I suddenly find myself as a teacher again. My main activity is to be surrounded by students. To show up at classes. To prepare. I'm finally doing the type of part-time teaching I had dreamed of as a young writer—small memoir classes—a salon of sorts—not packed community college classes with loads of papers, but I'm doing too much of it. Some weeks, I only go to the Grotto to write for one day instead of two. And I'm paying for two days a week. This is what I love—to write—but my writing is again taking back stage. Am I really retired? Or retired in the way I want to be retired? One day, at Notre Dame University where I teach a graduate creative writing class, I'm in the cafeteria before the 6:00 p.m. class, downing a cup of vegetable soup and a cup of coffee. Even though I love my students and the small class of twelve feels luxurious compared to thirty in each of my City College classes, I bemoan how late the class will go. I don't like driving on the freeway in the dark anymore, especially at 10:00 p.m. at night. Sometimes, when I enter the pitch-black parking lot, I gaze longingly at the bus that leaves and wonder if I could get on that bus. Could it just take me home? But, it doesn't go to San Francisco. I get into my car, turn on the heat, and leave campus for the freeway.

The lines on the road disappear at points, and I feel moments of panic, something I haven't felt in years. My hands are clammy, my breathing shallow. I scream to the steering wheel, "Panic, begone!" As I drive home, I stare at focal points, the signs on the road. I phonetically spell out the words: Millbrae, Serramonte, like a Montessori child learning sounds. I pray that there is a car in front of me that I can follow as my eyes don't adjust well to the dark. Night-blindness. My father had it. As I get closer to San Francisco, I see the strange Flintstone looking house and then statue of Junípero Serra, his finger pointed toward the freeway. I can make all of this out even in the dark. Then I see something red splattered across the road—a huge can of paint? Blood? I push that thought away as it couldn't be blood as I see it every time I drive by. When I pass the red splotch, I'm home free. The lights on the road are easy to follow, the landmarks visible. As much as I'm grateful my friend offered me this amazing job with money I need, I wonder what am I doing.

Also, all the money I make disappears as quickly as it appears. The money feels like it gets sucked into a black hole like the Bermuda Triangle. Maybe, I finally need to get one of those tracking money programs on the computer.

I check my credits/debits, and debits seem to take over. All this work and nothing to show for it? I haven't even lived extravagantly at all. I don't even go out to eat at medium-priced restaurants. I rarely get theater tickets or go to the ballet. But, I have a roof over my head. I have food to eat. A lot of people in this world don't have either of those things. What am I complaining about?

When more rentals happen for our room, on a short-term basis, our money situation looks up. People flood in from Europe, China, and Montreal. We buy bulk croissants from the local grocery store and good jam and butter, French roast coffee, and teas for the breakfast part of their stay. I set the table nicely. Some of them want to talk, and we learn about small towns in Norway, neighborhoods in Canada. We have artists, business people, and retirees finally on adventures they had put off for twenty or thirty years as they raised children. It's the beginning of a solution to our money woes and allows me to slowly divest of my teaching. I stop teaching at Notre Dame and later give up my women's literature class. I no longer spend three days a week preparing for that class.

Although renting out a room gives us extra income, we need more for our bills and helping our younger daughter in grad school. We decide to rent out the whole house and either stay with friends or stay in one room we have downstairs, through the chaotic basement mess. It takes about three months to get the house in top shape. We move precious objects to Jim's art room—a portrait Laura sandblasted of herself as a little girl, an antique chess set of the serfs against the royalty. But, the fixing is endless. The burners on the stovetop don't always line up, a potential fire hazard. Jim sticks cork in the bottom of them and then prays. A year later, we finally order a new stovetop. For the next couple of years, Jim and I rent out our whole house for ninety days a year, what's allowed under the new San Francisco law. Although I keep the one teaching job at UC Berkeley, private classes at my house, and two morning classes at the Grotto, I let go of my other classes. Jim is happy I'm not driving home in the dark, late at night. I can finally be more of a writer, more of what I want to be.

Betsy E. had a similar experience of getting overwhelmed in the first year and a half after retirement, though she wasn't working for money. Her husband is still working, and they paid off their mortgage a while ago. Their daughter, now a lawyer, is launched. After retirement, Betsy got involved in about six different community projects and wanted to do all of them well. She has a long history of working in the community, a highly respected and diligent worker. Everyone wanted Betsy on their team. Her input became crucial to each project. But after a couple of years, she felt overwhelmed. "I realized I needed to take more time for myself. I had a psychological change. I wanted more free days. Now I'm getting better at it, but it was hard to realize I couldn't do everything." She cites E.B. White who said, "I arise in the morning torn between a desire to improve the world and a desire to enjoy the world. This makes it hard to plan the day." She has now decided to spend at least some time, enjoying the day.

Although many people retire and still need to earn money—especially in the baby boomer generation of few pensions—a number of people I interviewed had planned well for retirement. They had not succumbed to all the refinance frenzy. They budgeted throughout their lives, earned enough money to live the life they wanted to live, inherited money, or worked with fee-only financial advisors such as Jennifer Lane, and were always able to pay down their debts.

However, even though they had enough money, some wanted to go back to their place of work for one or two days a week or find something similar and liked having a paycheck. John R. continues to see patients once a week. Steve initially took on two consulting jobs and helped two clubs get out of massive debt. He also got paid well, but it was tiring. Now he is not doing outside work at all and thinks about being an ESL teacher or doing volunteer work at the Veterans Administration hospital.

It's important to not take on too much right away. The fear of the void can motivate people to endlessly fill their days with activities and forget about the dreams they have for their retirement.

Jim, retired for a number of years without going back to work, except for the endless work on the house, has recently become a history teacher, something he was planning to be as a young man. He gets great adulation and praise from his students. "I'm finally using my history degree," he beams. He brings in extra money and revels in the material.

In December of my second year retired from City College our dog, Penny, died at sixteen years old. We were all on the phone at one point, Jim and I calling from the vet, Sarah crying in LA, Laura crying in Vermont, and Jim and I sobbing. Her death was sudden and unexpected. Laura, our younger daughter, was coming home from grad school the next day and hadn't seen her dog in over six months. "Why didn't she wait one more day at least," Laura asked the next day as she sat on her bed, tears soaking her face. The house was devastatingly empty without her. I remember seeing her shape for days, her soft white fur, her little whine, the smell of her dog breath as she stood at the top of the stairs, waiting and waiting. But, she was gone. Penny was the first dog I had ever had. She had been with our family for sixteen years. I cried on and off for at least a month, missing her every moment I was home. Her death affected me so deeply that for many days I still talked to her. Once, when I saw a vision of her by the landing of the stairs, as if waiting for her family to come home, I said, "Penny, it's okay. We'll be fine. You can go now." I never saw her at the landing again.

YEAR THREE

How do you reclaim your original retirement plan
for a balanced life filled with what makes you happy?
Are you good to yourself? Why is it important to be
flexible, never knowing what life will bring?

In May of 2016, Jim and I went on a trip to Paris and the South of France. Although Jim had been to Italy only seven years before with his brother and family, I hadn't been to Europe for eighteen years. After we did a house trade, I longed to go every year. My cousin, who travels often, said, "Many people don't travel much after seventy-five." What she said haunted me. If not now, when? We had enough miles for two tickets and a generous offer to stay in Paris with a friend.

Months before, on a trip home from visiting Oregon, we stopped at a Denny's restaurant. "What are five places you'd like to visit before you die?" I asked Jim as he ate his senior meal, an omelet and hash browns. He also downed some black coffee, more fuel for the road. We each picked five places and then picked France and England first, as places we agreed on. At nineteen, I had lived in France as part of a junior year abroad program—a pivotal year for me. I wanted to return, a nostalgia trip for that crazy phase of life. I had also started a book about that time.

When Jim and I finally went to France in May, we met up with Ken and his partner, Ed. Jim and I stayed with Catou in Paris. Ken, Catou, and I had all been students and became intensely close in Aix during my junior year abroad. We continued to stay in touch, now almost forty years later. My fluent French was not so fluent as Jim and I navigated the Paris metro and as we got lost, I fumbled at times with French, but I knew the challenge was good for both of us. The art we saw in Paris and at a new museum in Marseille was spectacular. We even saw the dolls Picasso made for his small children. One of the highlights of the trip was taking a ferry-ride to the island of Porquerolles. Catou had lived there part-time, and Ken and I had visited her house there so many years ago in our youthful bodies. Ken took Jim and me on gorgeous hikes, and we breathed in the scent of the turquoise sea and looked at the rock formations. Later, we walked on the soft white sand. We had made it to Europe.

Our next trip is to England. Jim, who thought he was Irish for many years, signed up on one of those ancestry websites and found out he's English! My grandmother was English, and it turns out our families come from places quite near to each other. Returning to England will also be an ancestry trip for us. As a nine-year old, after my parents received a settlement from their burns—my mother called it "burn money"—we all went to Europe. We visited my Aunt Ivy in Exeter. I remember her parrot, Polly, who said nursery rhymes, naturally with an English accent and how sometimes, when eating breakfast, she would make the sounds of bombs dropping, a shrieking sound, not pleasant as we ate our oatmeal and hoped it would be a sunny day. Polly had lived through World War II. Aunt Ivy also had a cross-eyed cat, Dinky. She took my sister, Annie, and me to the moors, and we watched her paint landscapes among the heather. I wanted to return to that part of England. While online the other night, I finally found the cemetery where my Jewish grandparents and uncle are buried— Mount Judah cemetery. We had never visited the cemetery when we were young. Perhaps the pain of his mother, father, and brother all dying so young was too much for my father to bear. Now, I want to go there on our next trip to New York, reconnect with parts of my ancestry, finally say Kaddish—the Jewish prayer for the dead—for the relatives I never met, yet who eternally remain part of my DNA. These trips are important.

"You can't take your money with you." That becomes more poignant as we age. Who knows how long we'll be able to move as well as we do.

It is now the end of the summer. Jim is home preparing for a history class. His students love him, but this is a new class at a new facility. Seeing him, I can remember all those first class jitters. At one point, a few months ago, he spent too much time preparing for the classes, and I wondered if the stress would be too difficult for him. Now, he has a method that works. He is learning how to balance prepping for classes with relaxation. He still runs at least twice a week. He is also still the handyman, installing a new stovetop so we don't have to worry about the burners when we rent out the house.

We have decided to slow down considerably on the short-term rentals. Our financial situation is much better. Our children both have good jobs and though they are still setting up their own savings accounts and have ancient cars, they recently received raises and are becoming completely independent. We have also decided, finally, to get a new dog. Even though most people think it's a crazy idea as Jim and I are both older, we know a new dog will bring us much happiness. And happiness is what we're after. How long do we have to live? We don't know. "Dogs lower your blood pressure," Sarah reminds us.

I've been writing almost every day lately, though that will soon slow down. I go in faithfully to the Grotto and now have a number of friends there, people I can talk to about all the important things in life. I teach there, go to Grotto parties and readings, and revel in the community. I still keep up with friends from City College; however, that is one thing I want to work on in the next year, making more regular dates with friends. As we're in our house more, we can have people over for dinner. Perhaps it's time to create Expression Night at our house again, invite people over for a monthly creative evening and potluck. I can also, finally, offer my house for meetings of my book club.

Today, I'm sitting at my local coffee shop writing, a five-block walk down Bosworth Street from home, rolling my suitcase that holds a few books and my computer. Glen Park Village, our neighborhood, has exploded with restaurants, a new library, market, and coffee shops over the last few years. Where I sit now, a family-run, neighborhood treasure has been here for many years. You can eat the best crepes in town, from pesto to alla Milanese. The owner recently opened an Italian restaurant across the street and runs back and forth between the two. He always says hello and goodbye to anyone entering and leaving. The ceiling is hung with huge burlap coffee sacks, the bulletin board filled with photos and flyers. They just added Wi-Fi recently, but many who come here seem to truly want to talk to each other. They are not screen-zombies, ensconced in screen worlds. People talk across old round wooden tables, dark knots of wood, light spots of wear and tear. Only a couple of people have computers on. At the moment, two strollers encircle two sleeping babies. It is 2:00 pm. I can do exactly what I want to do: take my computer to my favorite neighborhood cafe and write. I can stare out the window for as long as I want, watching cars turn down Diamond Street, dogs stroll by attached to owners, and now two women lean on a parking meter, talking intensely. City College, always in my heart, started yesterday— classes, meetings, syllabi, scared students, excited students—the grand machinery of a huge urban community college with the new semester revving up again. It's been two and a half years since I've been there for the first meeting day: coffee and donuts at the truck, schmoozing with friends and acquaintances then rushing back to my office to prepare, prepare, prepare. The first day of classes was always daunting, often meeting 100 students. Despite the pressure of needing to do part-time work, including renting out our house, I have no regrets of leaving when I did. I knew it was time.

Just a month ago, I wrote down my calming and health goals on a piece of paper and put it on the refrigerator. That has really helped. I've popped the right vitamins, joined the City College gym and swimming pool, and most days do my self-hypnosis tape. Sometimes, Jim and I lie on our backs and hold hands as we fall asleep, listening to a tape given to me when I had foot surgery four months ago. It is a restorative tape. As I fall asleep, I'm surrounded by white light, healing light. All the sore places truly feel better the next morning. I'm a huge believer in these tapes and in relaxation or in meditation. John L., who began meditation after he retired, says he tries different things on different days. Taking a walk in the park can be a type of meditation.

We pick up our puppy in a month. Since I have asthma and allergies, we had to go to a breeder. We received photos when they were first born and yesterday a photo with their eyes open. Six of them, Bichon Frise puppies with small ears and black noses, cuddle together for warmth on a brown rug. We've already picked out a name: Ella. When we got Penny, Jim and I were both working, and Sarah and Laura were ten and twelve. With more time now, I find I'm reading puppy books and learning facts like a puppy's eyes take twenty-four hours to open. The breeder has sent us a list of things to buy. One is a small stuffed toy that can be heated up for Ella's first night at our home, a warm cuddly toy on her first night away from her mama. I know we might both be sleep deprived, but it will be worth it.

What next? I know I'll continue to write but I might take a break for a while. Maybe do more hiking and even camping. It's months since Jim and I have spent time outdoors. Like most people in the twenty-first century, we need to disconnect from the Internet and cellphones and connect with the earth and the stars.

I'm sure some wonderful things and difficult things will happen over the next years as Jim and I get older. I keep working on my anxiety, doing something calming a few times a day whether it's a short walk or getting together with a friend—an everyday commitment to take care of my body, mind, and soul works wonders. Staying calm will give me resilience to face both personal struggles and also what is going on the world. Some days, I need to turn off the news.

Connections with others do sustain us as Dr. Chandra said. My family comes first; talking with my children and seeing them as much as possible gives me great pleasure. Friends are important, too, and I want to work on more regular get-togethers with friends in the next year. Our next trip will probably be a visit back east to see family, and then we hope to go to England. However, what is most important is what we do everyday, whether it's a walk in Glen Park, a meal with a friend, volunteering to tutor in an after-school program, planning a potluck with neighbors, watching a favorite TV show, actively creating art, writing, or simply lying down and putting on a hypnosis tape, luxuriating in being able to relax midafternoon.

Through all the changes that will surely come during the retirement phase of life, what is crucial is that we remain flexible and stay kind to ourselves and to each other, knowing we are making important choices for our unique body, mind, and soul. As we live to the end of our lives, we can feel proud of what we leave to the others who will surely follow. We have been here on this earth. We have worked and we have loved.

I finish writing at the cafe, pack up, and walk the five blocks home.

Also Available from Central Recovery Press

Behavioral Health

Breaking the Trance: A Practical Guide for Parenting the Screen-Dependent Child
George Lynn, MA, LMHC with Cynthia C. Johnson, MA •
$16.95 US • ISBN: 978-1-942094-26-5 • E-book: 978-1-
942094-27-2

Real Hope, True Freedom: Understanding and Coping with Sex Addiction
Milton S. Magness, DMin and Marsha Means, MA • $17.95 US •
ISBN: 978-1-942094-30-2 • E-book: 978-1-942094-31-9

Self-Acceptance: The Key to Recovery from Mental Illness
Victor Ashear, PhD with Vanessa Hastings • $24.95 US •
ISBN: 978-1-937612-91-7 • E-book: 978-1-937612-92-4

Engage the Group, Engage the Brain: 100 Experiential Activities for Addiction Treatment
Kay Colbert, LCSW and Roxanna Erickson-Klein, PhD, LPC
• $26.95 US • ISBN: 978-1-937612-89-4 • E-book: 978-1-
937612-90-0

Irrelationship: How We Use Dysfunctional Relationships to Hide from Intimacy
Mark Borg, Jr., PhD; Grant Brenner, MD; Daniel Berry, RN, MHA • $16.95 US • ISBN: 978-1-942094-00-5 • E-book: 978-1-942094-01-2

All Bets Are Off: Losers, Liars, and Recovery from Gambling Addiction
Arnie and Sheila Wexler with Steve Jacobson • $16.95 US • ISBN: 978-1-937612-75-7 • E-book: 978-1-937612-76-4

Wisdom from the Couch: Knowing and Growing Yourself from the Inside Out
Jennifer L. Kunst, PhD • $16.95 US • ISBN: 978-1-937612-61-0 • E-book: 978-1-937612-62-7

Hard to Love: Understanding and Overcoming Male Borderline Personality Disorder
Joseph Nowinski, PhD • $15.95 US • ISBN: 978-1-937612-57-3 • E-book: 978-1-937612-58-0

Many Faces, One Voice: Secrets from The Anonymous People
Bud Mikhitarian • $17.95 US • ISBN: 978-1-937612-93-1 • E-book: 978-1-937612-94-8

A Man's Way through Relationships: Learning to Love and Be Loved
Dan Griffin, MA • $15.95 US • ISBN: 978-1-937612-66-5 • E-book: 978-1-937612-67-2

Disentangle: When You've Lost Your Self in Someone Else
Nancy L. Johnston, MS, LPC, LSATP • $15.95 US • ISBN: 978-1-936290-03-1 • E-book: 978-1-936290-49-9

Game Plan: A Man's Guide to Achieving Emotional Fitness
Alan P. Lyme; David J. Powell, PhD; Stephen R. Andrew, LCSW •
$15.95 US • ISBN: 978-1-936290-96-3 • E-book: 978-1-
937612-04-7

The Light Side of the Moon: Reclaiming Your Lost Potential
Ditta M. Oliker, PhD • $16.95 US • ISBN: 978-1-936290-95-6 •
E-book: 978-1-937612-03-0

Inspirational

The Wisdom of a Meaningful Life: The Essence of Mindfulness
John Bruna • $15.95 US • ISBN: 978-1-942094-18-0 • E-book:
978-1-942094-19-7

*I Don't Know What to Believe: Making Spiritual Peace with
Your Religion*
Rabbi Ben Kamin • $16.95 US • ISBN: 978-1-942094-04-3 •
E-book: 978-1-942094-05-0

The Truth Begins with You: Reflections to Heal Your Spirit
Claudia Black, PhD • $17.95 US • ISBN: 978-1-936290-61-1 •
E-book: 978-1-936290-78-9

Caregiving

*Connecting in the Land of Dementia: Creative Activities to
Explore Together*
Deborah Shouse • $16.95 US • ISBN: 978-1-942094-24-1 •
E-book: 978-1-942094-25-8

The Family Caregiver's Manual: A Practical Planning Guide to Managing the Care of Your Loved One
David Levy, JD, Gerontologist • $24.95 US • ISBN: 978–1–942094–12–8 • E-book: 978–1–942094–13–5

Love in the Land of Dementia: Finding Hope in the Caregiver's Journey
Deborah Shouse • $15.95 US • ISBN: 978–1–937612–49–8 • E-book: 978–1–937612–50–4

Dancing in the Dark: How to Take Care of Yourself When Someone You Love Is Depressed
Bernadette Stankard and Amy Viets • $15.95 US • ISBN: 978–1–936290–70–3 • E-book: 978–1–936290–83–3

Memoirs

Starved: A Nutrition Doctor's Journey from Empty to Full
Anne McTiernan, MD, PhD • $16.95 US • ISBN: 978–1–942094–28–9 • E-book: 978–1–942094–29–6

Never Leave Your Dead: A True Story of War Trauma, Murder, and Madness
Diane Cameron • $15.95 US • ISBN: 978–1–942094–16–6 • E-book: 978–1–942094–17–3

The Jaguar Man: A Memoir
Lara Naughton • $15.95 US • ISBN: 978–1–942094–20–3 • E-book: 978–1–942094–21–0

Bottled: A Mom's Guide to Early Recovery
Dana Bowman • $16.95 US • ISBN: 978–1–937612–97–9 • E-book: 978–1–937612–98–6

Body Punishment: OCD, Addiction, and Finding the Courage to Heal
Maggie Lamond Simone • $15.95 US • ISBN: 978-1-937612-81-8 • E-book: 978-1-937612-82-5

Weightless: My Life as a Fat Man and How I Escaped
Gregg McBride • $17.95 US • ISBN: 978-1-937612-69-6 • E-book: 978-1-937612-70-2

Acrobaddict
Joe Putignano • $17.95 US • ISBN: 978-1-937612-51-1 • E-book: 978-1-937612-52-8

Rage: The Legend of "Baseball Bill" Denehy
Bill Denehy with Peter Golenbock • $16.95 US • ISBN: 978-1-937612-55-9 • E-book: 978-1-937612-56-6

From Harvard to Hell . . . and Back: A Doctor's Journey through Addiction to Recovery
Sylvester "Skip" Sviokla III, MD with Kerry Zukus • $16.95 US • ISBN: 978-937612-29-0 • E-book: 978-1-937612-30-6

Dark Wine Waters: My Husband of a Thousand Joys and Sorrows
Fran Simone, PhD • $15.95 US • ISBN: 978-1-937612-64-1 • E-book: 978-1-937612-65-8

Finding a Purpose in the Pain: A Doctor's Approach to Addiction Recovery and Healing
James L Finley, Jr., MD • $15.95 US • ISBN: 978-1-936290-71-0 • E-book: 978-1-936290-84-0

The Mindful Addict: A Memoir of the Awakening of a Spirit
Tom Catton • $18.95 US • ISBN: 978-0-9818482-7-3 • E-book: 978-1-936290-44-4

Some Assembly Required: A Balanced Approach to Recovery from Addiction and Chronic Pain
Dan Mager, MSW • $16.95 US • ISBN: 978-1-937612-25-2 • E-book: 978-1-937612-26-9

Relationships and Recovery _____

Dirt Roads & Diner Pie: One Couple's Road Trip through Recovery from Childhood Sexual Abuse
Shonna Milliken Humphrey • $16.95 US • ISBN: 978-1-942094-22-7 • E-book: 978-1-942094-23-4

Making Peace with Your Plate: Eating Disorder Recovery
Robyn Cruze and Espra Andrus, LCSW • $16.95 US • ISBN: 978-1-937612-45-0 • E-book: 978-1-937612-46-7

Loving Our Addicted Daughters Back to Life: A Guidebook for Parents
Linda Dahl • $16.95 US • ISBN: 978-1-937612-85-6 • E-book: 978-1-937612-86-3

The Joey Song: A Mother's Story of Her Son's Addiction
Sandra Swenson • $15.95 US • ISBN: 978-1-937612-71-9 • E-book: 978-1-937612-72-6

Out of the Woods: A Woman's Guide to Long-Term Recovery
Diane Cameron • $15.95 US • ISBN: 978-1-937612-47-4 • E-book: 978-1-937612-48-1

May I Sit with You: A Simple Approach to Meditation
Tom Catton • $15.95 US • ISBN: 978-1-937612-83-2 • E-book: 978-1-937612-84-9

Reference

RecoveryMind Training: A Neuroscientific Approach to Treating Addiction
Paul H. Earley, MD, DFASAM • $24.95 US • ISBN: 978-1-942094-32-6 • E-book: 978-1-942094-33-3

Behavioral Addiction: Screening, Assessment, and Treatment
An-Pyng Sun, PhD; Larry Ashley, EdS; Lesley Dickson, MD • $18.95 US • ISBN: 978-1-936290-97-0 • E-book: 978-1-937612-05-4